THE PHOTOGRAPHY
OF
LEWIS CARROLL

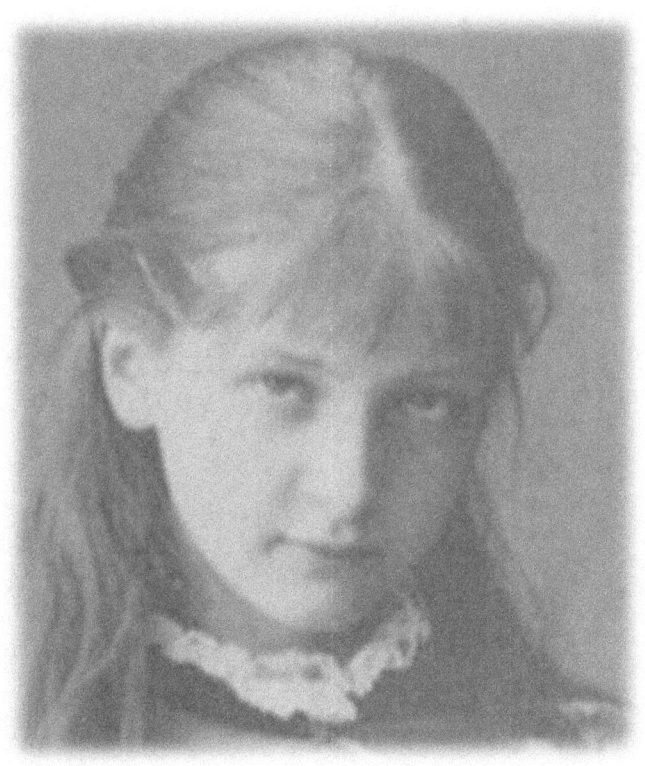

ANDREW G FREW

CONTENTS

INTRODUCTION

THE LIFE OF LEWIS CARROLL

THE PHOTOGRAPHY OF LEWIS CARROLL

76 PLATES

MEMOIR OF ISA BOWMAN

THE MAN BEHIND THE CAMERA

6 PLATES

QUOTATIONS FROM A SELECTION FROM THE LETTERS OF LEWIS CARROLL

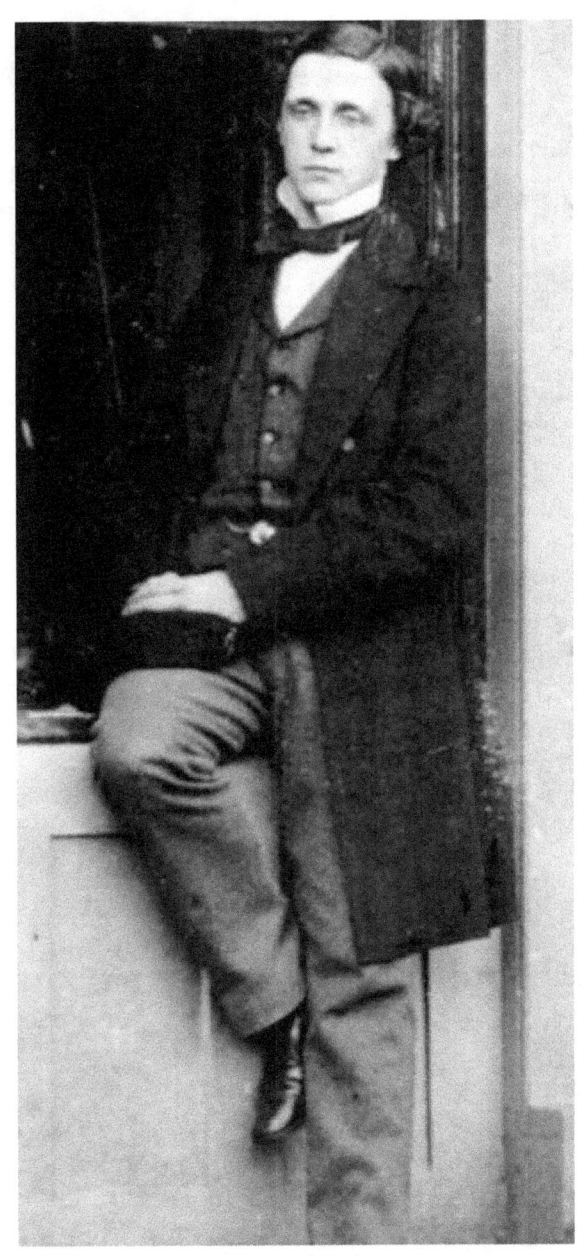
Lewis Carroll (1832-1898)

INTRODUCTION

Charles Dodgson aka Lewis Carroll was born on 27th January in 1832 he was typical of his revolutionary Aquarian sun sign though bound by the rules of society in latter life he changed completely into an enigma, a puzzle of a man far removed from his previous self, a genius for writing nonsense verse.

In 1855 Carroll took up his post as a mathematician at Christ Church, he had the pedigree and the talent, he spent his life there, teaching and writing and finding diversion in the art form of photography.

Influenced by his uncle Skeffington Lutwidge, Carroll took up **photography** in 1856 at the age of twenty-four.

The photographic technique he used was the collodion wet plate process, whereby a glass plate was coated with a mixture of soluble iodide and collodion, submerged in a silver nitrate solution in a dark room, then exposed in the camera while still wet, producing a glass negative from which multiple prints could be made.

Carroll took hundreds of portraits in his career. The most well known are of upper middle class children, but he also photographed his friends, colleagues, and many celebrities of the time.

His first photography revolves around the Liddell sisters including Alice Liddell, his 'ideal child-friend'. Not only did the young girl inspire his books' main character, she also modeled in theatrical as well as exotic costumes for many of his photographs. Shy and ill at ease among adults, Carroll preferred the company of children and especially young girls, half of his 3000 photographs do represent young girls.

Today, his photographs can fetch between £1,000 and £40,000 at auction – fans of Lewis Carroll and of early Victorian photography are both keen buyers. There might have been many more available, yet Carroll reputedly destroyed many of them.

His most famous photos, of course, are the infamous ones—his portraits of young girls, some of them in today's morals are controversial for occasionally he took them in the nude—which have caused decades of speculation about his sexual proclivities.

His affection for younger girls, many of whom inspired the stories he wrote, has led many to conclude that Carroll may very well have been a suppressed pedophile. There has never been any evidence of this until an uncovering of a photo found in a museum in France. It shows a photo of one of his most intimate friends.

Carroll stopped taking photographs in 1880 in order to focus on writing and other academic pursuits. But his decades in photography were quite productive. He is considered one of the early masters of the photographic art.

Carroll's empathy for the emotions of childhood is part of what gives the "Alice" books their energy; they approximate how bewildering and curious the world can seem through a young person's eyes. When Carroll looked through the lens of his Victorian camera, what he saw was through the looking glass the world upside down, much like the world of Alice. It feels fitting to picture Lewis Carroll spending his leisure hours looking at an up-side down topsy-turvy world and then, with the trick of his camera, turning it back around.

This selection is contentious there are few pictures of famous people; few of the adults of the world he felt uncomfortable with, but many more of whom inspired his beautiful writing.

THE LIFE OF LEWIS CARROLL

Charles Dodgson had spent his very early life secluded in the parsonage of Daresbury. His father was a man of the Church. He no doubt wanted his son to follows his footsteps. His nature was quite, and unassuming the young Charles was indeed well suited to his future role to be, in the Church. From the first he had an imaginative and inventive mind he counted, snails, toads and small animals among his friends. All these memories of his early days of youth he returned to in his writing under the pseudonym Lewis Carroll. From the first he was anxious to learn mathematics. Once he presented a book of logarithms to his father, with the request, 'Please explain.' His father retorted, you too young to understand about the subject. He heard his father, but asked once again, 'Please explain.' He had a logical and mechanical brain that enjoyed working out puzzles he was very fond of invention and used his innate abilities to entertain his ten brothers and sisters. He constructed a train from a wheel barrow to the joy of his siblings. He was also a clever conjuror, doing magical tricks and he made all kinds of puppets with all the strings attached. When he reached twelve he was sent to school at Richmond and the letters he wrote home have survived he wrote of his friends he made and of his experiences at the school and they reveal he enjoyed the company of his peers. He wrote to his sisters:

'My dear Fanny and Memy,—I hope you are all getting on well, as also the sweet twins, the boys I think that I like the best, are Harry Austin, and all the Tates of which there are 7 besides a little girl who came down to dinner the first day, but not since, and I also like Edmund Tremlet, and William and Edward Swire, Tremlet is a sharp little fellow about 7 years old, the youngest in the school, I also like Kemp and Mawley. The rest of the boys that I know are Bertram, Harry and Dick Wilson, and two Robinsons, I will tell you all about them when I return.'

Yr affec' brother Charles.

After leaving Richmond at the age of 14 he was sent to Rugby School in 1846 a very different experience he learnt to grow up pretty quickly athletic prowess was highly regarded there and Charles admittedly was not a great athlete, but he shined in his studies particularly in the field of mathematics and his upright conduct was especially noted by his teachers. On reflection he acknowledged his educational advancement at Rugby School but hated the general system of writing out impositions, in other words copiously copying from the black board. He made just one friend there which underlines that he had undergone a certain amount of deprivation in terms of social compatibility. After completing three years he left and in 1851 he started academic studies at Christ Church the same college attended previously by his father. He was to live there for the rest of his life taking residence in the college. He obtained First Class Honours in Mathematics and a Second in Classical Moderations. He was recommended for student ship whose criteria was, he not marry while he held the post.

In 1855 he took up his post as a mathematician eight years after the birth of Harry Liddell the first child of the Dean of Christ Church. He would soon meet Harry and following on from this meet all the Dean's subsequent progeny, Lorina, Alice and Edith, the three girls that would accompany him on a boat trip to Godstow, one late Friday summer afternoon and recount the story of 'Alice's Adventures Underground.' .I have no doubt he was beloved by the girls, he was witty, and attractive with a non serious demure when in their company. In 1856 he had taken up the new art form of photography and many of the plates in this book come from this period of his sittings with the Liddell girls. His passion for the art is evident in the care he took not only over the process for it was a demanding development process but in his subjects.

In 1865 he published 'Alice in Wonderland,' a tale whose inspiration he forged from his boat trip with the Liddell girls. The book became a public success. He was inundated with the admiration of many new child friends. Many of whom are found immortalised in the photographic plates in this book.

He went on to write a sequel too 'Alice in Wonderland,' in 'Alice through the Looking-Glass,' and followed it up with further children writings, such as 'The Hunting of the Snark,' 'Phantasmagoria,' 'Sylvie and Bruno,' and many more. But he never achieved greater fame than that bequeathed Alice his creation, based on the real Alice Liddell. A masterwork in the genre of nonsense writing that children, love to read today.

Carroll continued to photograph until 1880 when suddenly he stopped. Perhaps he was tired of the format or may have been getting himself into trouble, for he was reproached for photographing his subject's nude, notably by their parents. Carroll died in 1898, departing the world that had become so weary, maybe in age or realisation perhaps of his own quote,

'Is all our Life, then, but a dream?'"

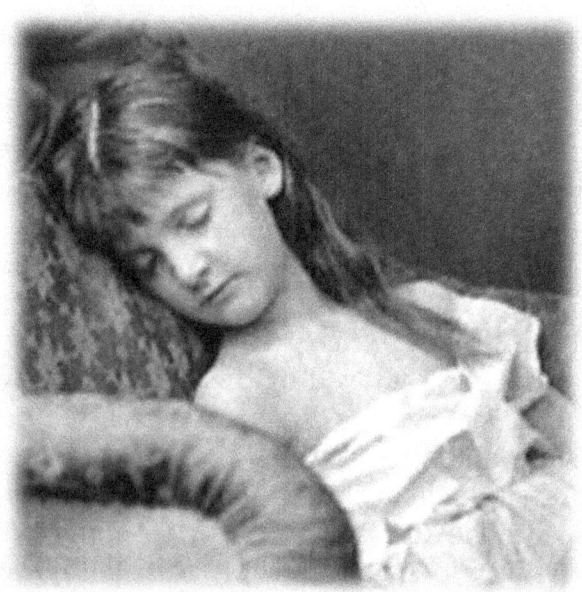

Alexandra 'Xie' Rhoda Kitchin (b.1864-1925)

Photographed by Lewis Carroll

THE PHOTOGRAPHY OF LEWIS CARROLL

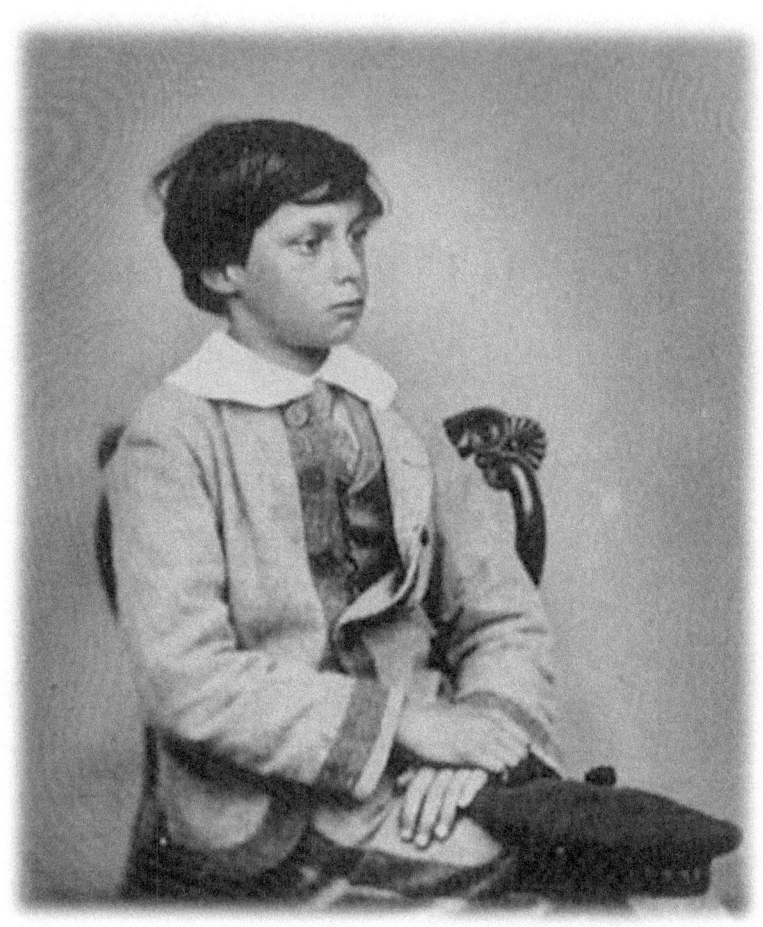

Harry Liddell (b.1847)

Carroll photographed just about anything that could be photographed, including Harry Liddell, the young son of the new dean at Christ Church college. Eventually he would meet the Liddell girls, Lorina, Alice and Edith.

He wrote in his diary on June 3: "Spent the morning at the Deanery, photographing the children."

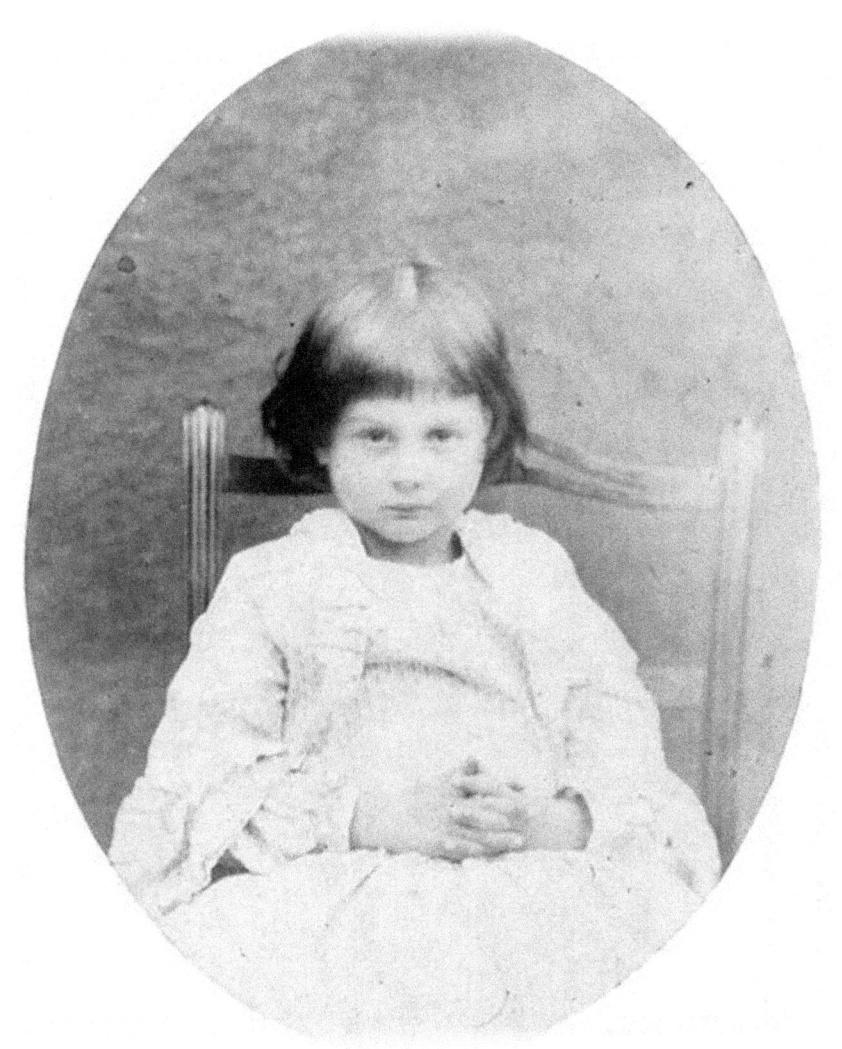

Alice Liddell, June 1857

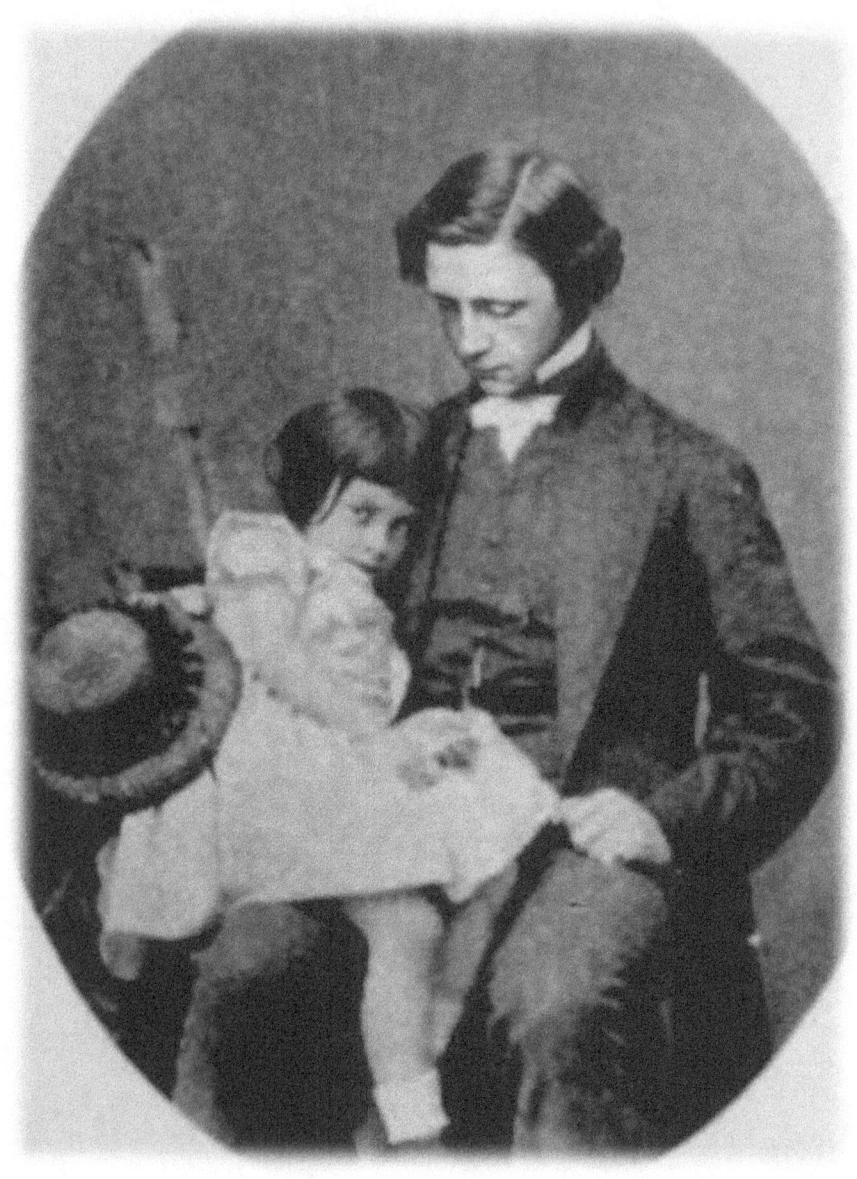

Alice Liddell and Lewis Carroll

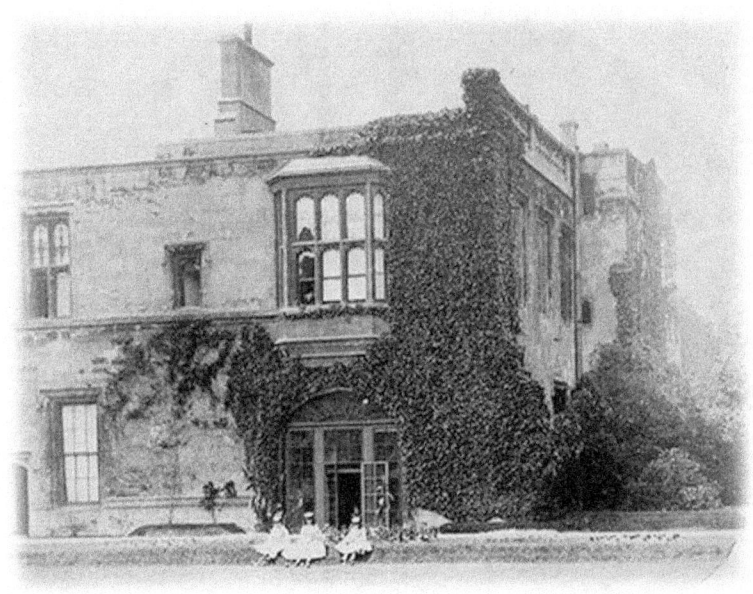

Alice, Lorina and Edith in the Deanery garden

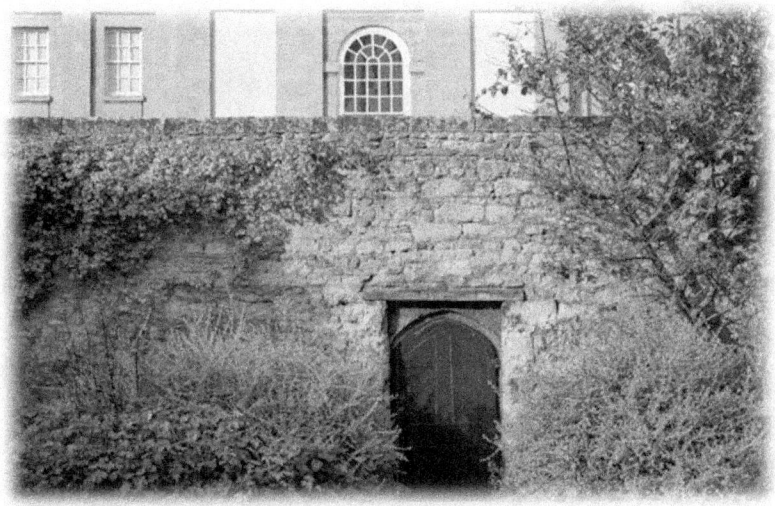

The door between the dean's private garden it's the door little Alice would generally have found locked

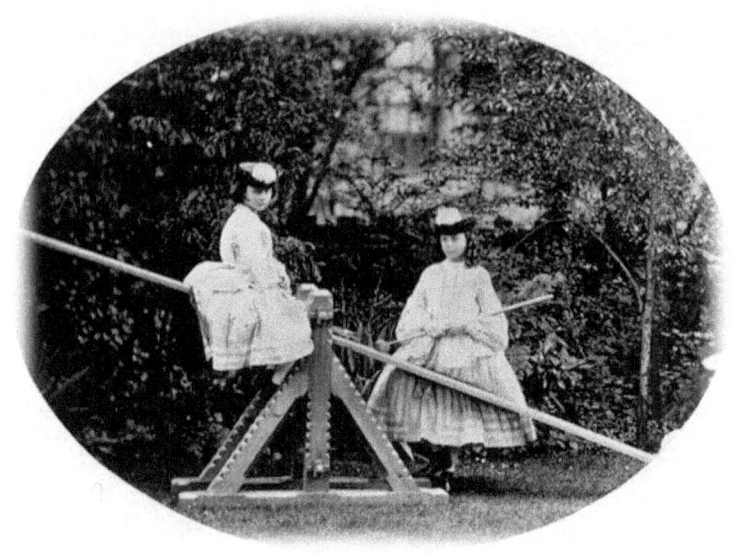

Alice and Lorina Liddell

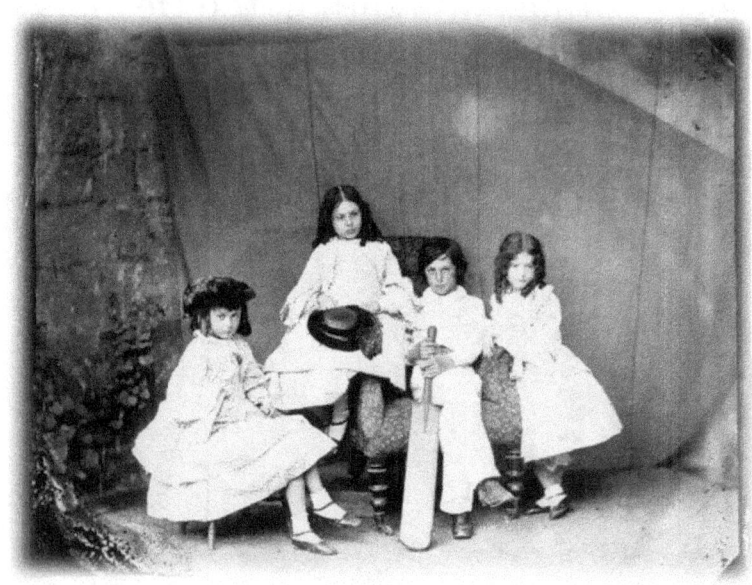

Alice, Lorina, Harry and Edith Liddell

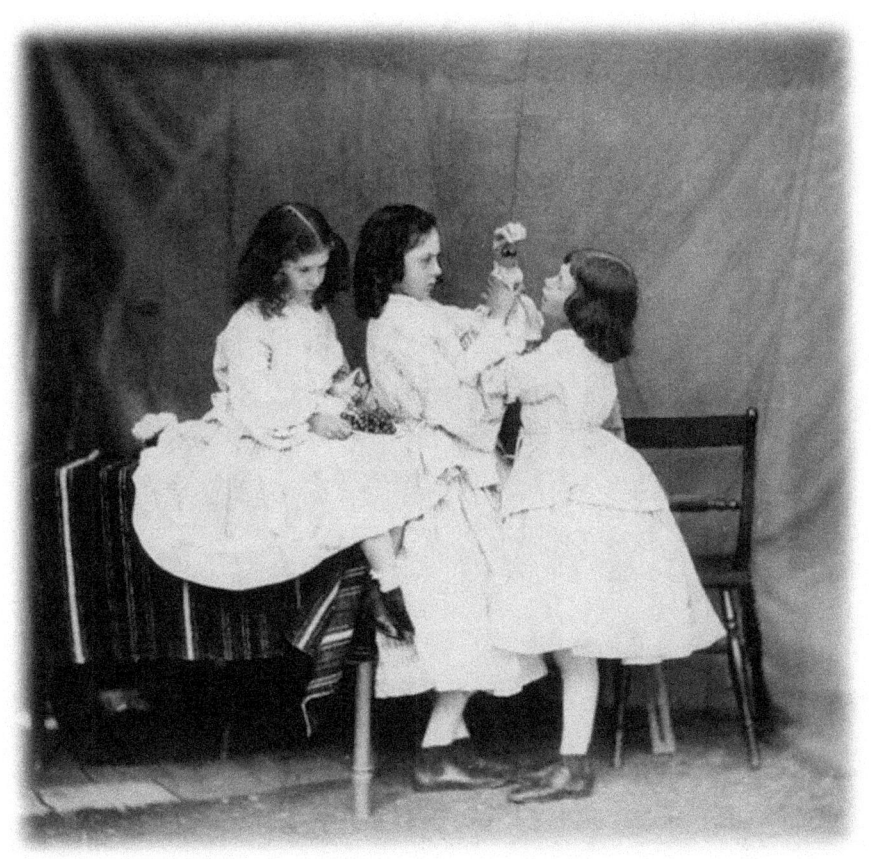

Edith, Lorina and Alice Liddell

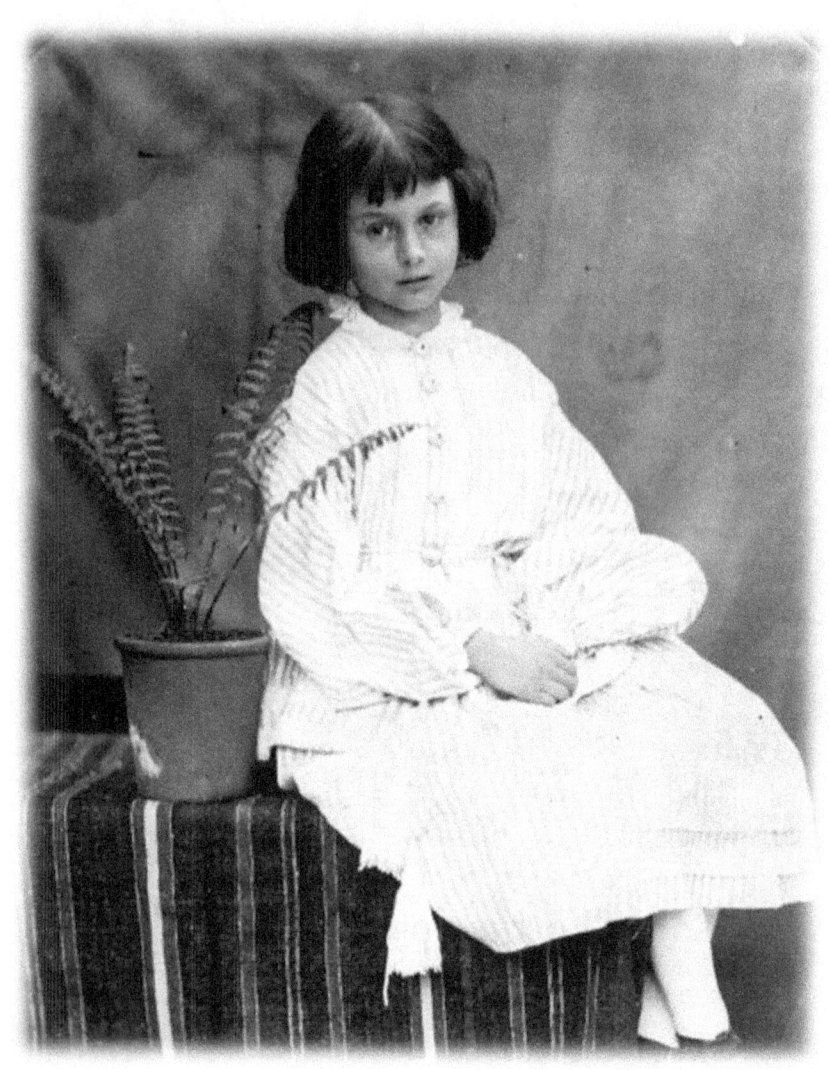
Alice Liddell (b.1852)

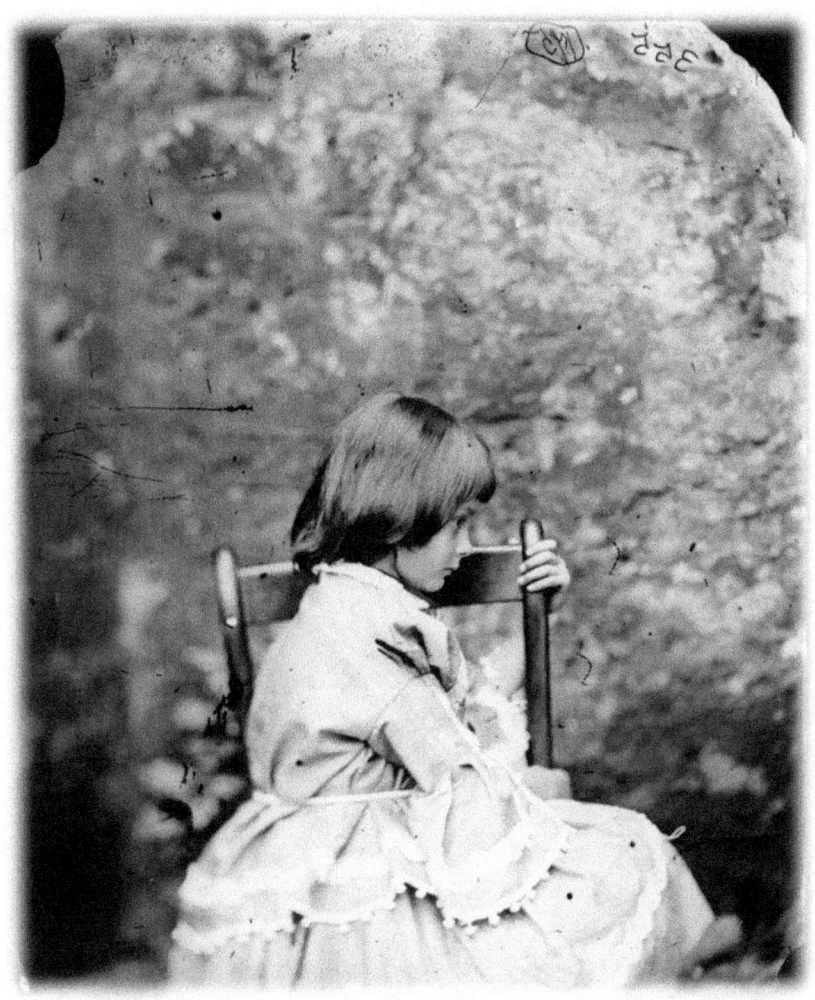

Alice Liddell, summer 1858,

In profile against the sandstone wall in the Deanery garden at Christ Church

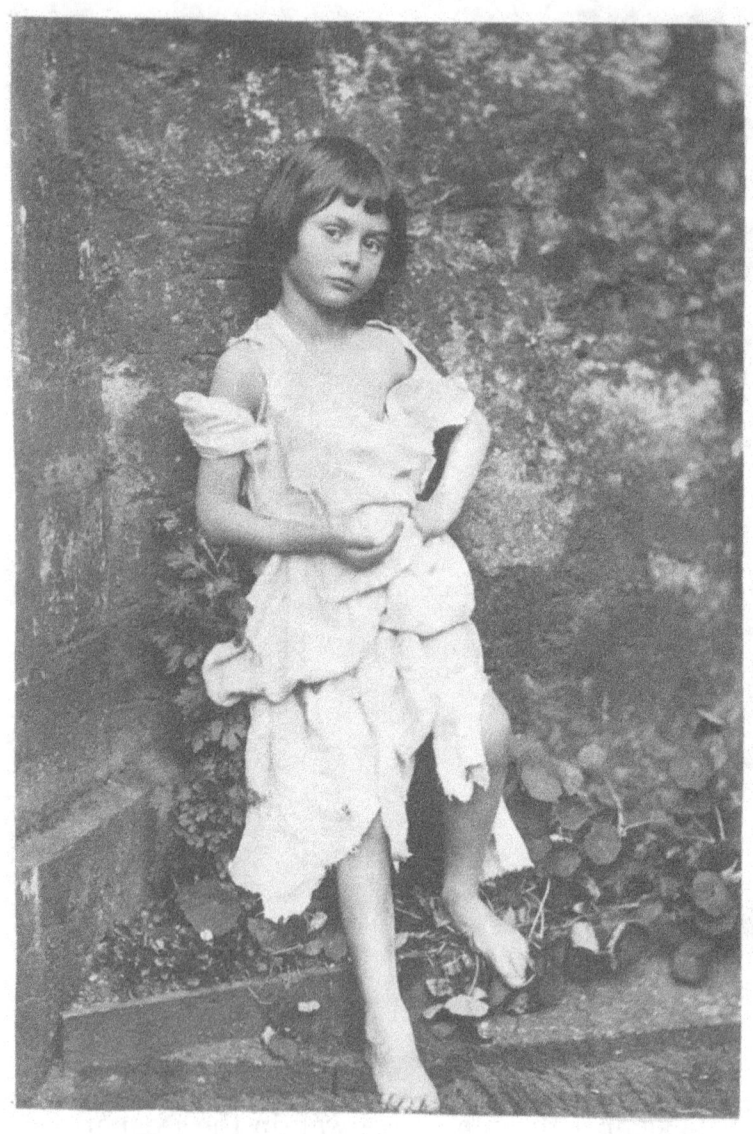

Alice Liddell as Beggar-Maid, Summer 1858.

Perhaps Carroll's most famous photo the dreamy eyes are childish in contrast to the come-hither posture, with Alice's rags slipping off her shoulder, revealing the left nipple; inspired by a Tennyson poem

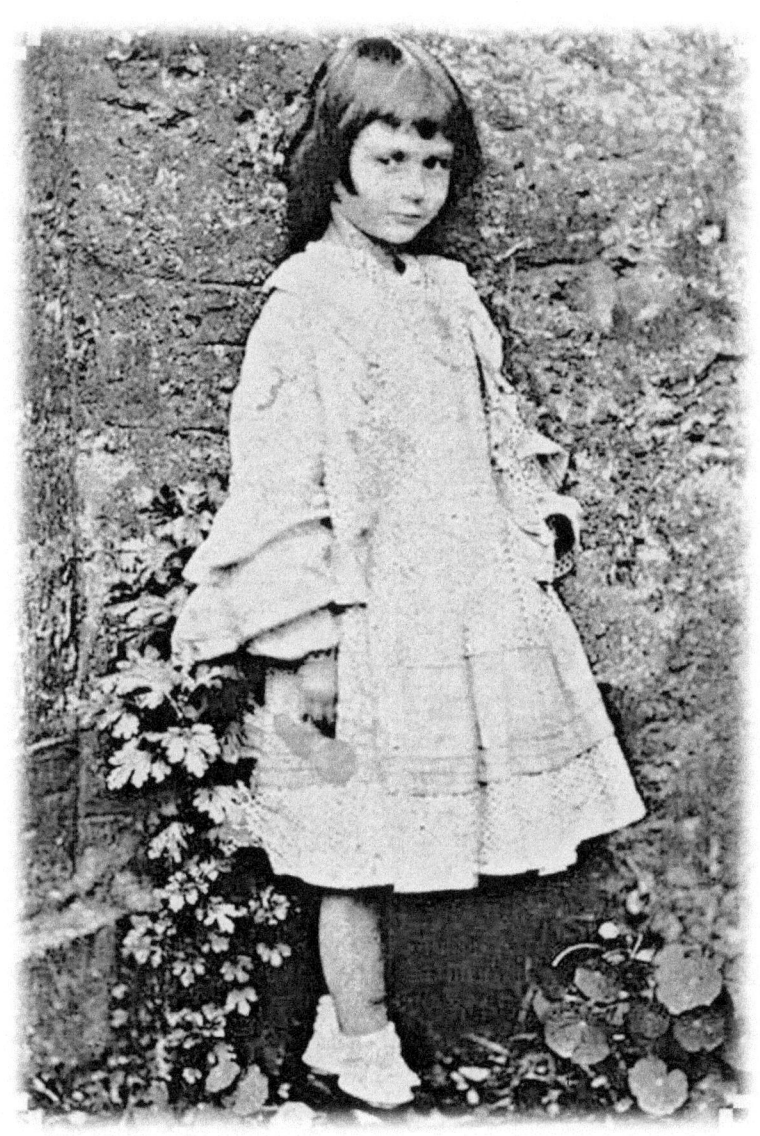
Alice Liddell (b.1852)

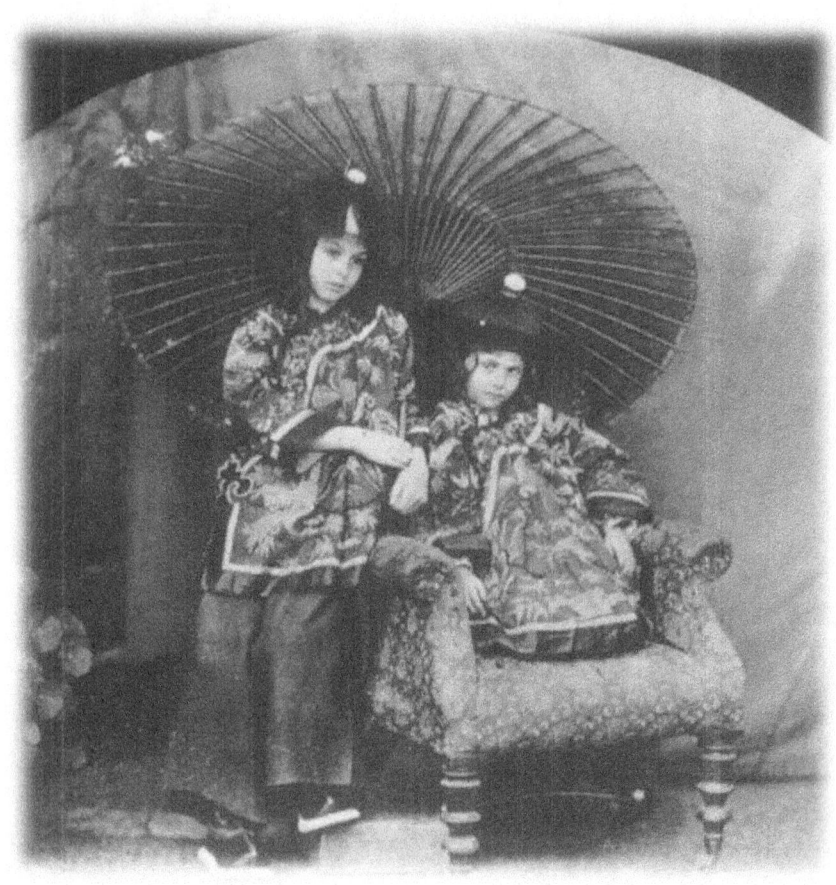

Lorina and Alice Liddell

Carroll first told the story of "Alice" July 4, 1862 while he, the three Liddell sisters (Lorina, 13; Alice, 10; Edith, 8), and Carroll's friend, Robinson Duckworth, rowed up the Isis river. Duckworth recalled that day in a letter to Collingwood:

"I rowed stroke and he rode bow in the famous Long Vacation voyage to Godstow when the three Miss Liddells were our passengers, and the story was actually composed and spoken over my shoulder for the benefit of Alice Liddell, who was acting as 'cox' of our gig. I remember turning round and saying, "Dodgson, is this an extempore romance of yours?" And he replied, "Yes, I'm inventing as we go along."

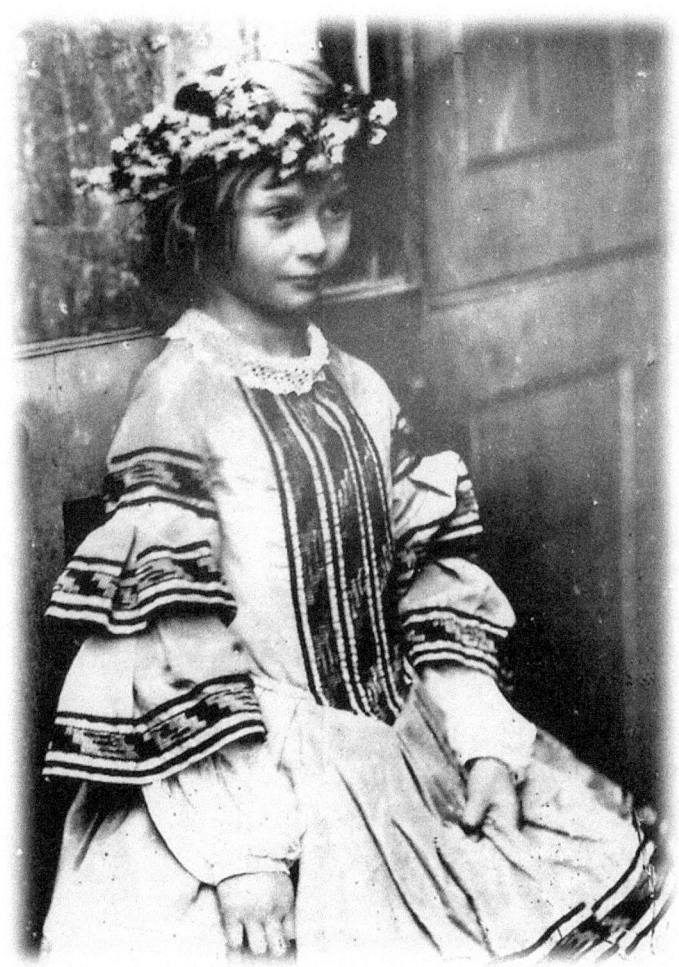

Alice Liddell

That evening Alice begged "Mr Dodgson" (the girls always addressed him so) to write down the story. He wrote an outline during a train trip to London the next day and began work on the famous manuscript copy on November 13.

Carroll's diary for 4th July 1862

July 4 (F) Atkinson brought over to
my rooms some friends of his, a Mrs.
& Miss Peters, of whom I took photographs,
& who afterwards looked over my albums
& staid to lunch. They then went off
to the Museum, & Duckworth & I
made an expedition up the river to
Godstow with the 3 Liddells: we
had tea on the bank there, & did
not reach Ch. Ch. Again till ¼
past 8, when we took them on to
my rooms to see my collection of
micro-photographs, & restored them to
the Deanery just before 9

July 5 (Sat.) Left, with Atkinson,
for London at 9.. 2, meeting at the
station the LIddells, who went along by the
same train. We reached 4, Alfred
Place about 11, & found Aunt [Lucy, Frances],
& [Elizabeth] there, & took the 2 last to see
Marochetti's studio. After luncheon
Atkinson left, & we visited the Inter-
-national Bazaar.

[Carroll's addition to the July 4 entry, on the left-hand page:]

On which occasion I told
them the fairy-tale of "Alice's
Adventures Under Ground," which I
undertook to write out for Alice,
& which is now finished (as to the
text) though the pictures are not
yet nearly done—Feb. 10. 1863
nor yet—Mar. 12. 1864.
"Alice's Hour in Elfland"? June 9/64.
"~~Alice's~~ Adventures in Wonderland"? June 28.

There is an acrostic poem at the end of *Through the Looking-Glass*. Reading downward, taking the first letter of each line, spells out Liddell's full name. The poem has no title in *Through the Looking-Glass*, but is usually referred to by its first line, "A Boat Beneath a Sunny Sky".

A boat beneath a sunny sky,
Lingering onward dreamily
In an evening of July--

Children three that nestle near,
Eager eye and willing ear,
Pleased a simple tale to hear--

Long has paled that sunny sky:
Echoes fade and memories die.
Autumn frosts have slain July.

Still she haunts me, phantomwise,
Alice moving under skies
Never seen by waking eyes.

Children yet, the tale to hear,
Eager eye and willing ear,
Lovingly shall nestle near.

In a Wonderland they lie,
Dreaming as the days go by,
Dreaming as the summers die:

Ever drifting down the stream--
Lingering in the golden gleam--
Life, what is it but a dream?

ALICE'S ADVENTURES IN WONDERLAND, was published July 4, 1865, having been expanded to twice its original length, and with Carroll's charming illustrations replaced by those of John Tenniel.

Carroll visited the Liddell's far more frequently in 1863 than in previous years: "Destined to meet the Liddell's perpetually just now..." he wrote in his diary February 17, 1863. He visited the Deanery 10 times in April, 9 times in May, and 8 times in June. That's when the mysterious split occurred. Carroll was supposed to use the girls to court the governess but it appeared he was using the governess to court Alice or her elder sister Lorina. In any case Mrs Liddell had enough.

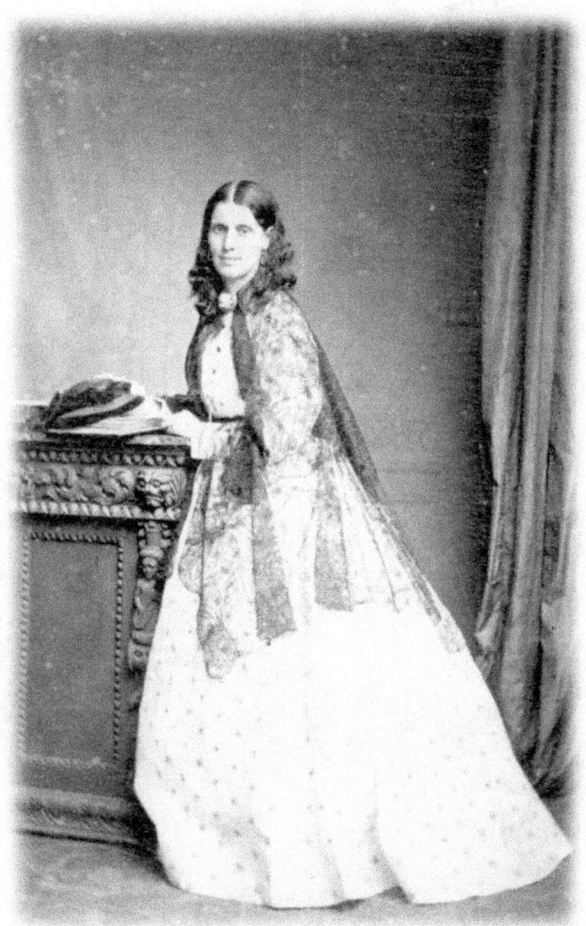

Mrs Liddell aka 'Kingfisher'

Mrs Liddell called 'Kingfisher' as she sought her daughters alliances with royalty tore up all of Carroll's letters to Alice.

In an article published in CORNHILL MAGAZINE (July 1932) Alice said,

"I cannot remember what any of them were like, but it is an awful thought to contemplate what may have perished in the Deanery waste-paper basket."

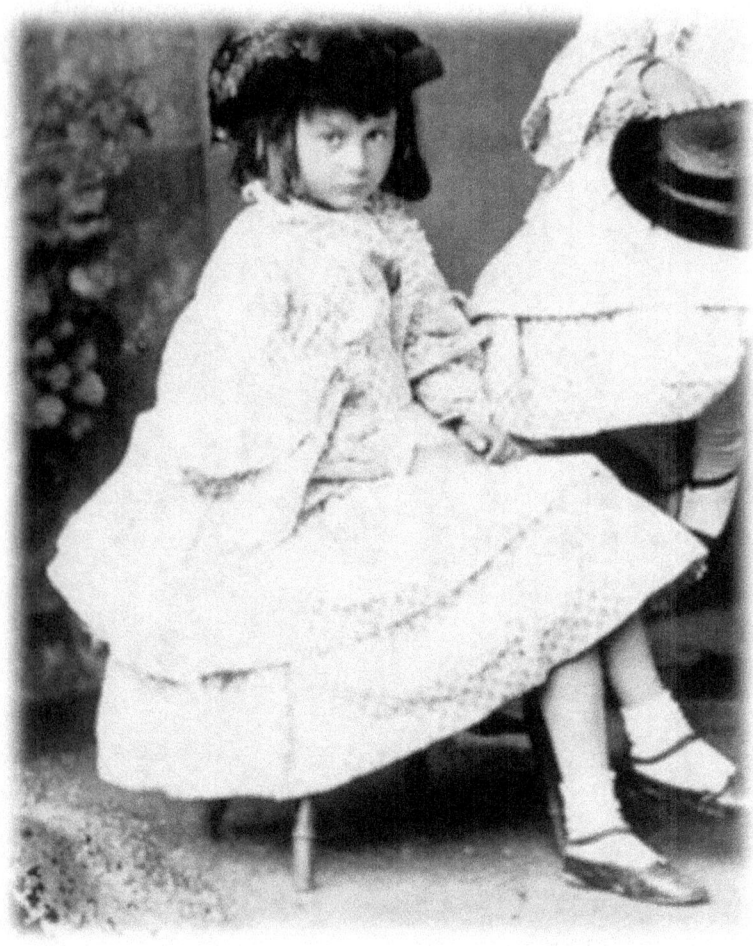

Alice Liddell (b.1852)

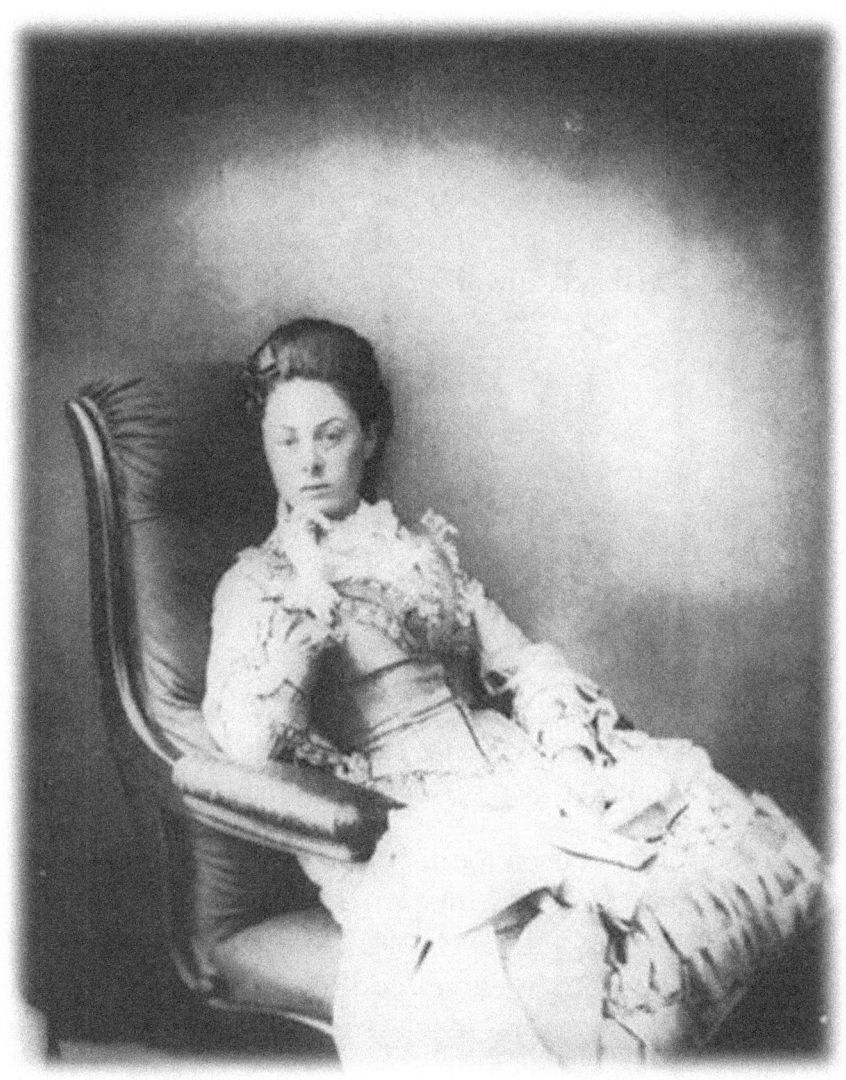

Lorina 'Ina' Liddell (b.1849)

Lorina wrote two letters to Alice regarding her conversation with Florence Becker Lennon about the 1863 split between Carroll and the Liddells. In the second letter, written May 2, 1930, Lorina said,

"I suppose you don't remember when Mr. Dodgson ceased coming to the Deanery? How old were you? I said his manner became too affectionate to you as you grew older and that mother spoke to him about it, and that offended him so he ceased coming to visit us again, as one had to give some reason for all intercourse ceasing. I don't think you could have been more than 9 or 10 on account of my age! I must put it a bit differently for Mrs. B's book. I had no idea my words were to be taken down!"

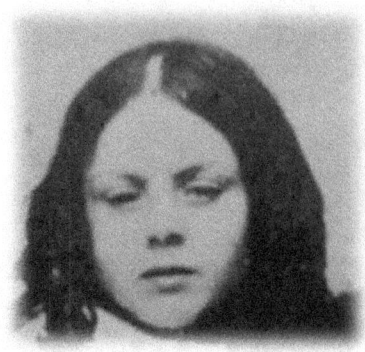

It is possible that Lorina was not telling all to her sister Alice or letting on about her own special relationship with Carroll.

In 1996, Karoline Leach found what became known as the "Cut pages in diary" document— a note allegedly written by Charles Dodgson's niece, Violet Dodgson, summarizing the missing page from 27–29 June 1863, apparently written before she (or her sister Menella) removed the page. The note reads:

"L.C. learns from Mrs. Liddell that he is supposed to be using the children as a means of paying court to the governess — he is also supposed soon to be courting Ina". (Leach, 1999)

This might imply that the break between Carroll and the Liddell family was in fact caused by concern over alleged gossip linking Carroll to "Ina" (Alice's older sister, Lorina). Carroll appears to have turned his romantic attentions from Alice to Lorina. Historical evidence suggests there was more occurring here, of strange things, a love triangle of Liddell's.

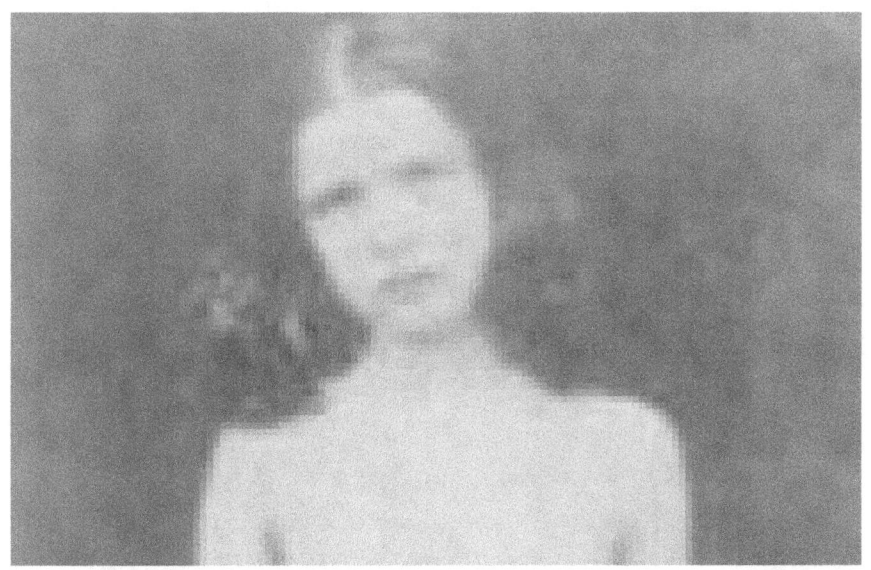

Lorina Liddell

A controversial photograph discovered by the BBC was found in a French museum with a note on the frame attributing it to Carroll showing the likeness of Lorina in the nude. Lorina would have been beyond the age considered for such a pose the childhood innocence Carroll promoted in photography. This explicit photograph could explain the reason for the rift that caused Carroll to break with the Liddell's in 1863, when Alice was 11 yrs and Lorina was a teenager of fourteen years.

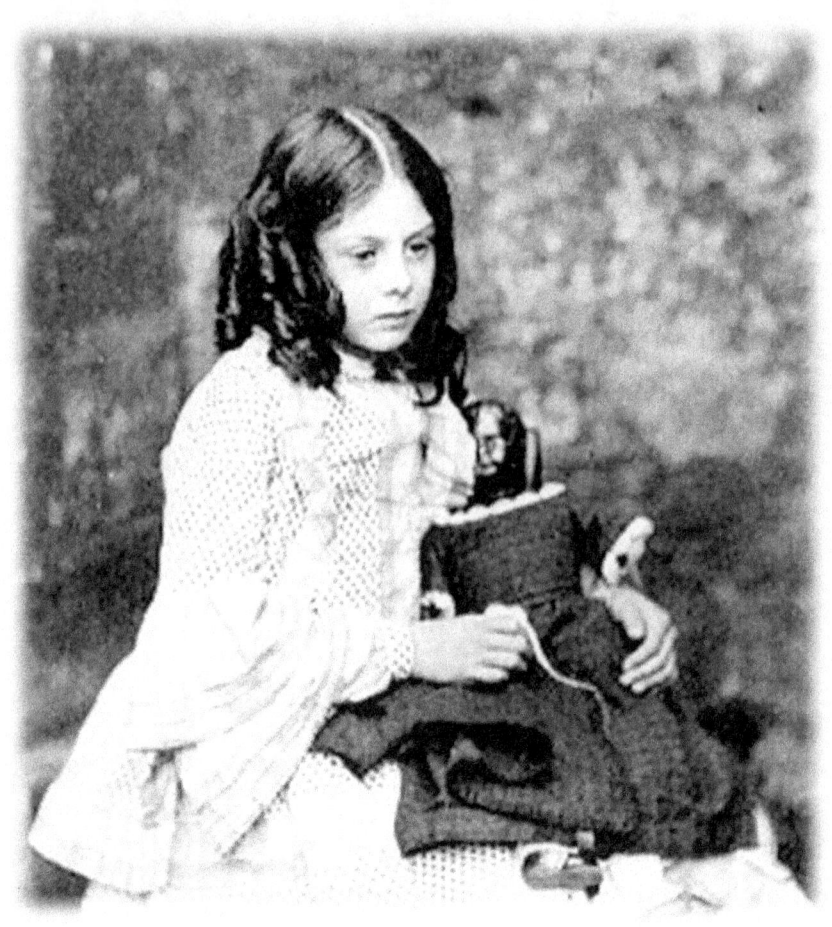

Lorina 'Ina' Liddell (b.1849)

Lorina became infatuated by Carroll

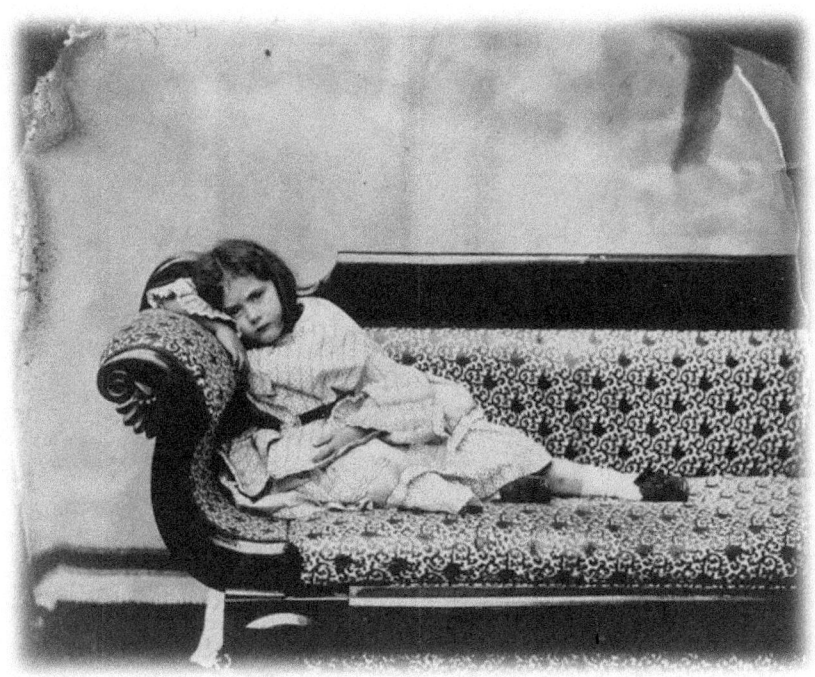

Edith Liddell 1860

Edith died June 26, 1876, at only 22 years old. Alice's son said, "She was the member of the family to whom my mother was especially devoted -- and to the day of her death nearly sixty years later she could hardly bear to speak of Edith's death."

Edith is portrayed as the Eaglet in the story of Alice in Wonderland. Some sources also report that she, not Alice, was used as a model for Carroll's original illustrations that he drew for Alice's Adventures Underground.

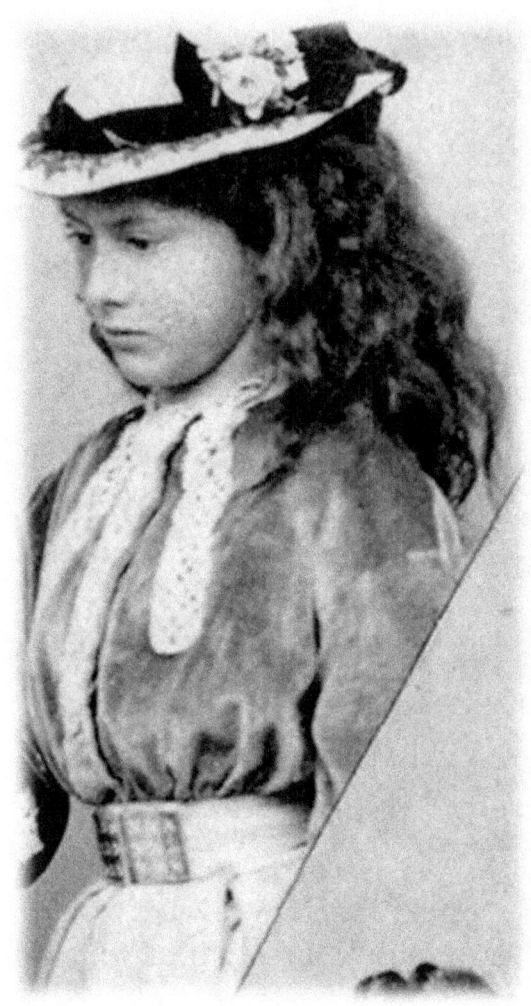

Edith Liddell (b. 1854)

Edith died in 1876, at the age of 22, shortly before she was to be married.

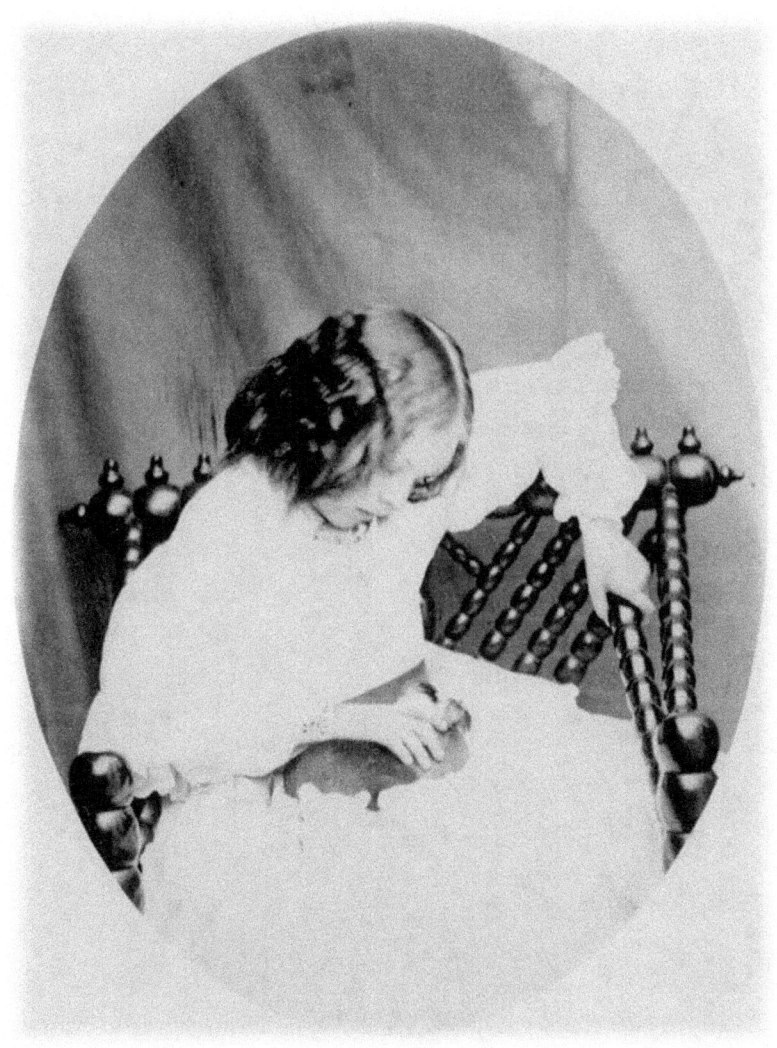

Bessie Slatter and pet guinea pig, 1862

He gave her inscribed copies of ALICE'S ADVENTURES IN WONDERLAND ("Bessie Slatter, from the Author"); THROUGH THE LOOKING-GLASS ("Elizabeth Anne Slatter, from the Author, Christmas, 1871"); and even EIGHT OR NINE WISE WORDS ABOUT LETTER-WRITING.

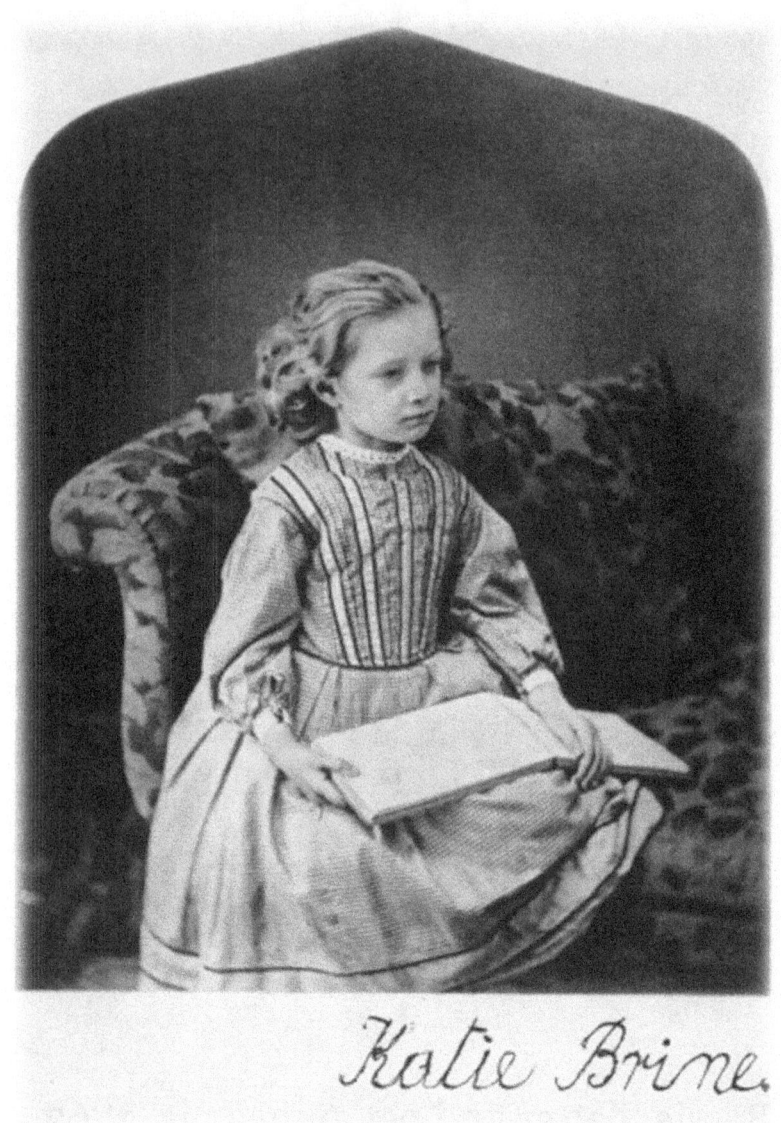

Katie Brine, June 16, 1866

Her grandfather, Dr. E. B. Pusey, nominated Carroll for Studentship for Christ Church, Christmas Eve, 1852

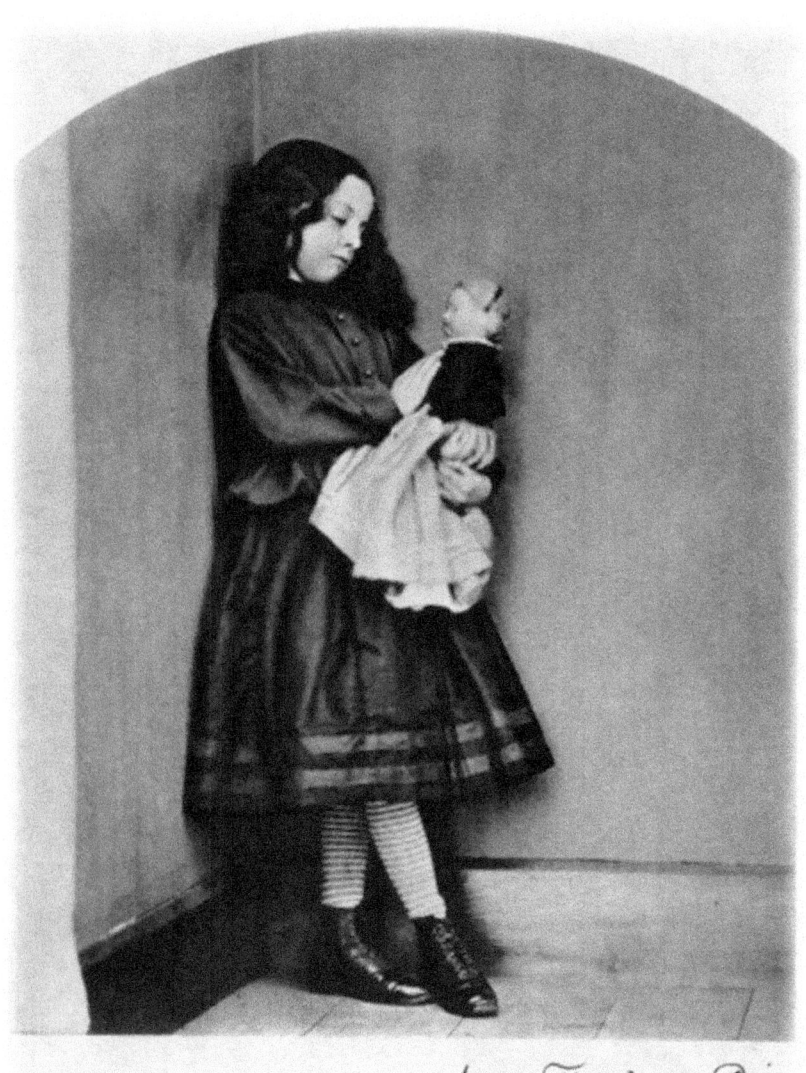

Agnes Florence Price, March 24, 1864

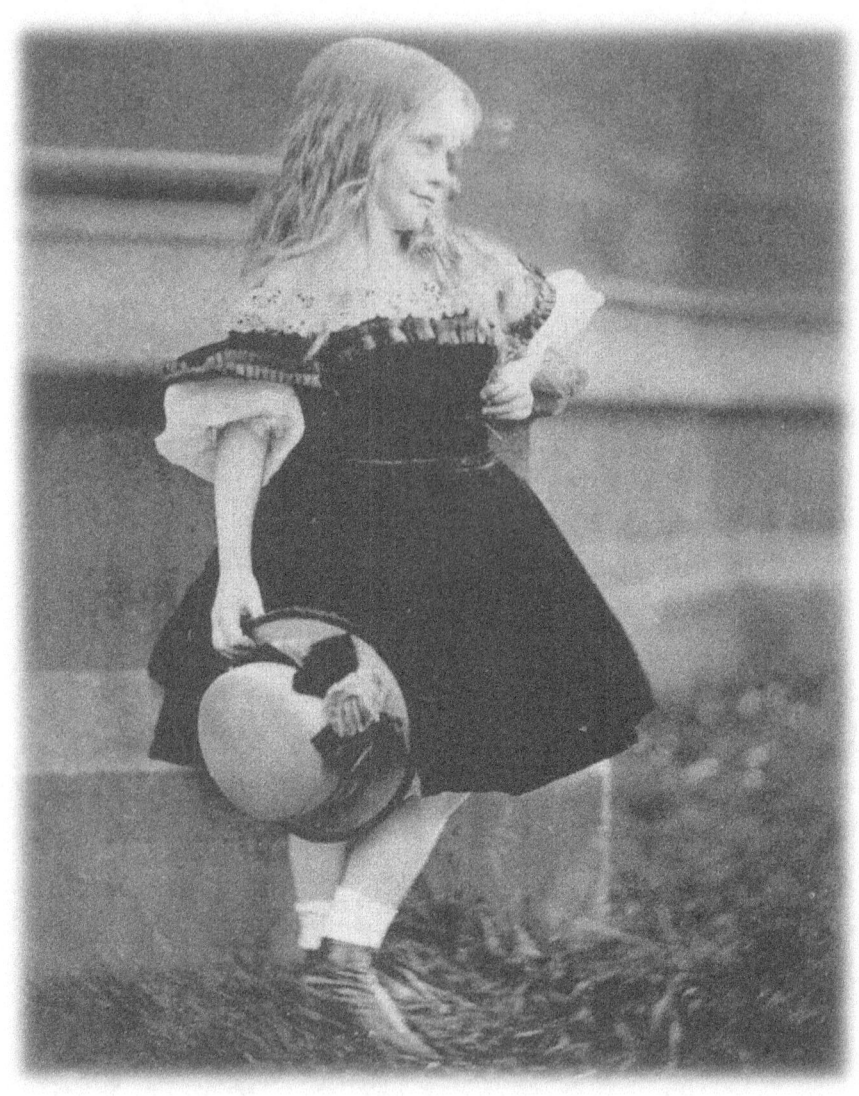

Beatrice Henley, September, 1862

BEATRICE.

In her eyes is the living light
Of a wanderer to earth
From a far celestial height:
Summers five are all the span—
Summers five since Time began
To veil in mists of human night
A shining angel-birth.

Does an angel look from her eyes?
Will she suddenly spring away,
And soar to her home in the skies?
Beatrice! Blessing and blessed to be!
Beatrice! Still, as I gaze on thee,
Visions of two sweet maids arise,
Whose life was of yesterday:

Of a Beatrice pale and stern,
With the lips of a dumb despair,
With the innocent eyes that yearn—
Yearn for the young sweet hours of life,
Far from sorrow and far from strife,
For the happy summers, that never return,
When the world seemed good and fair:

Of a Beatrice glorious, bright—
Of a sainted, ethereal maid,
Whose blue eyes are deep fountains of light,
Cheering the poet that broodeth apart,
Filling with gladness his desolate heart,
Like the moon when she shines thro' a cloudless night
On a world of silence and shade.

And the visions waver and faint,
And the visions vanish away
That my fancy delighted to paint—
She is here at my side, a living child,
With the glowing cheek and the tresses wild,
Nor death-pale martyr, nor radiant saint,

Yet stainless and bright as they.

For I think, if a grim wild beast
Were to come from his charnel-cave,
From his jungle-home in the East—
Stealthily creeping with bated breath,
Stealthily creeping with eyes of death—
He would all forget his dream of the feast,
And crouch at her feet a slave.

She would twine her hand in his mane:
She would prattle in silvery tone,
Like the tinkle of summer-rain—
Questioning him with her laughing eyes,
Questioning him with a glad surprise,
Till she caught from those fierce eyes again
The love that lit her own.

And be sure, if a savage heart,
In a mask of human guise,
Were to come on her here apart—
Bound for a dark and a deadly deed,
Hurrying past with pitiless speed—
He would suddenly falter and guiltily start
At the glance of her pure blue eyes.

Nay, be sure, if an angel fair,
A bright seraph undefiled,
Were to stoop from the trackless air,
Fain would she linger in glad amaze—
Lovingly linger to ponder and gaze,
With a sister's love and a sister's care,
On the happy, innocent child.

Dec. 4, 1862.

Lewis Carroll

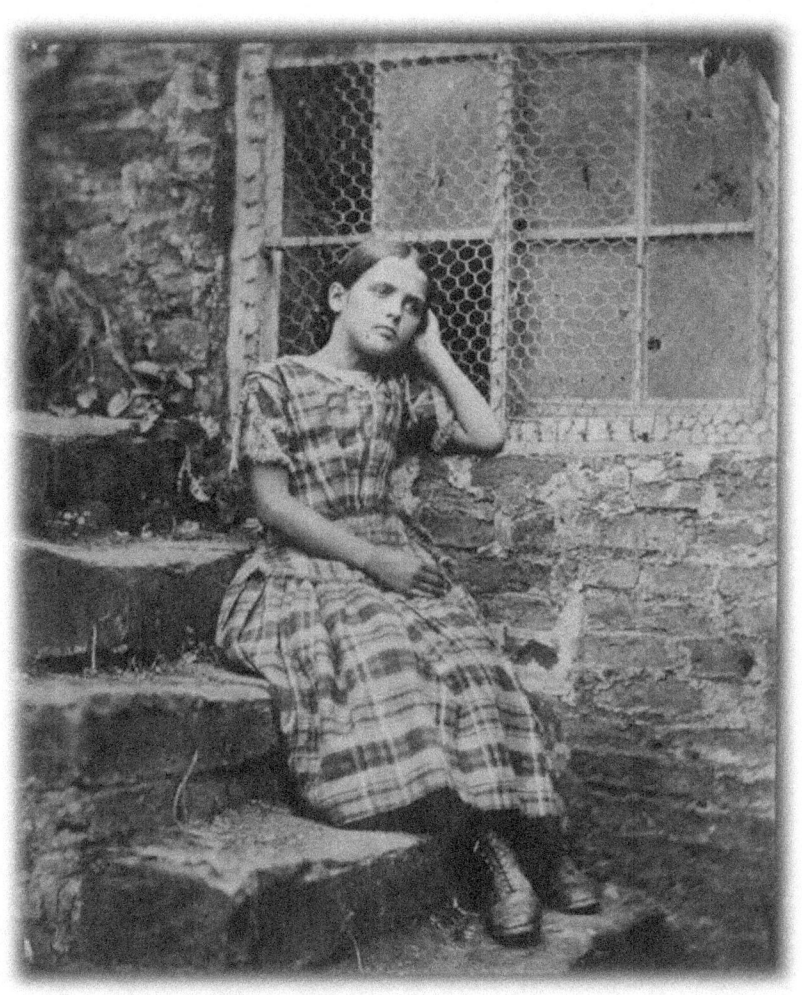

"Coates"; Annie Coates

She was the daughter of an employee at Croft Rectory, August 1857

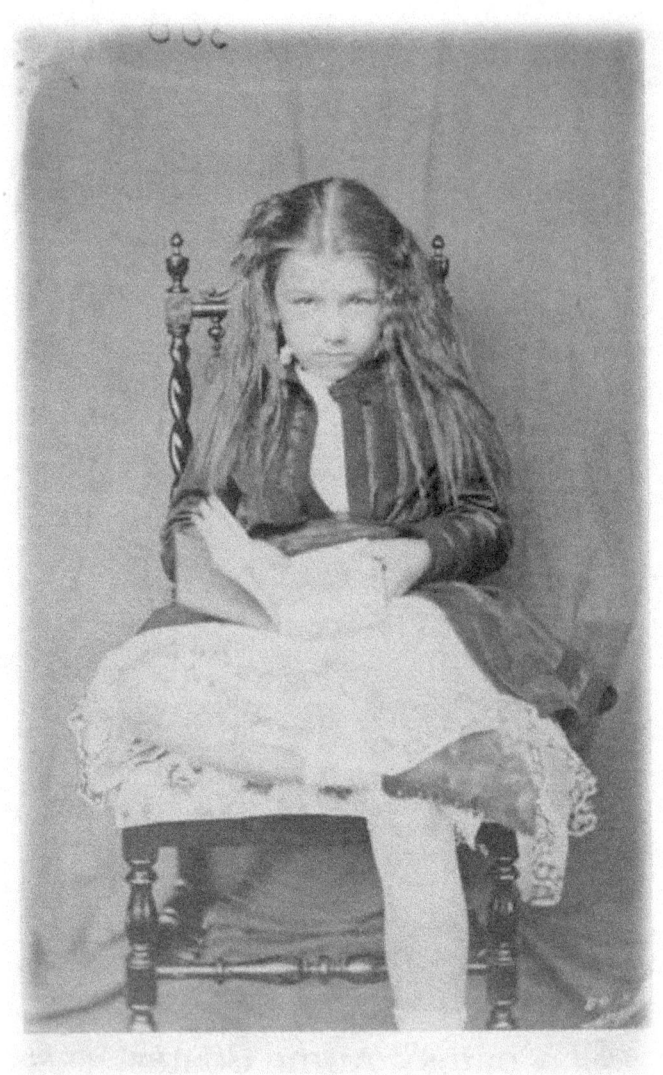

Isabella "Ella" Drury, September 1869.

Carroll had just met the Drury sisters, Ella, Emmie and Minnie, that year

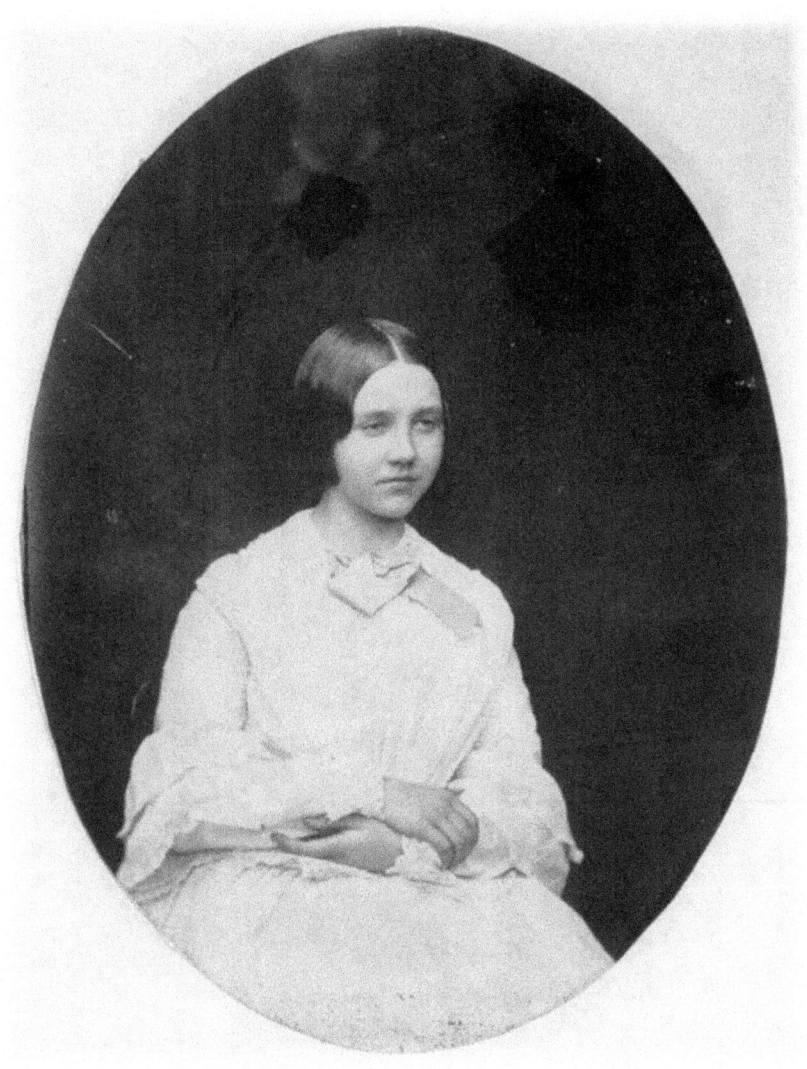

Lucy Hutchinson Tate (1856)

Carroll lived at the Tate residence, and wrote to two of his sisters on August 5, 1844 that "there are 7 besides a little girl who came down to dinner the first day, but not since..." Lucy (1842-1873) was the little girl he was referring to.

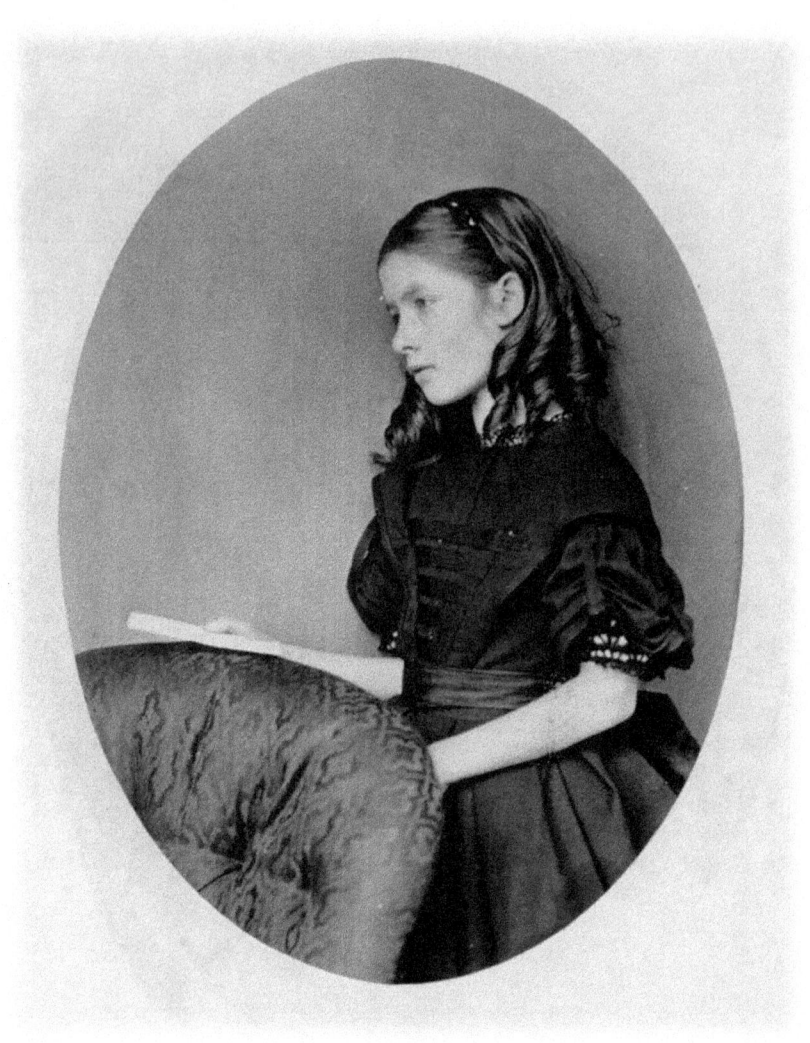

Bessie Goundry, June 1864

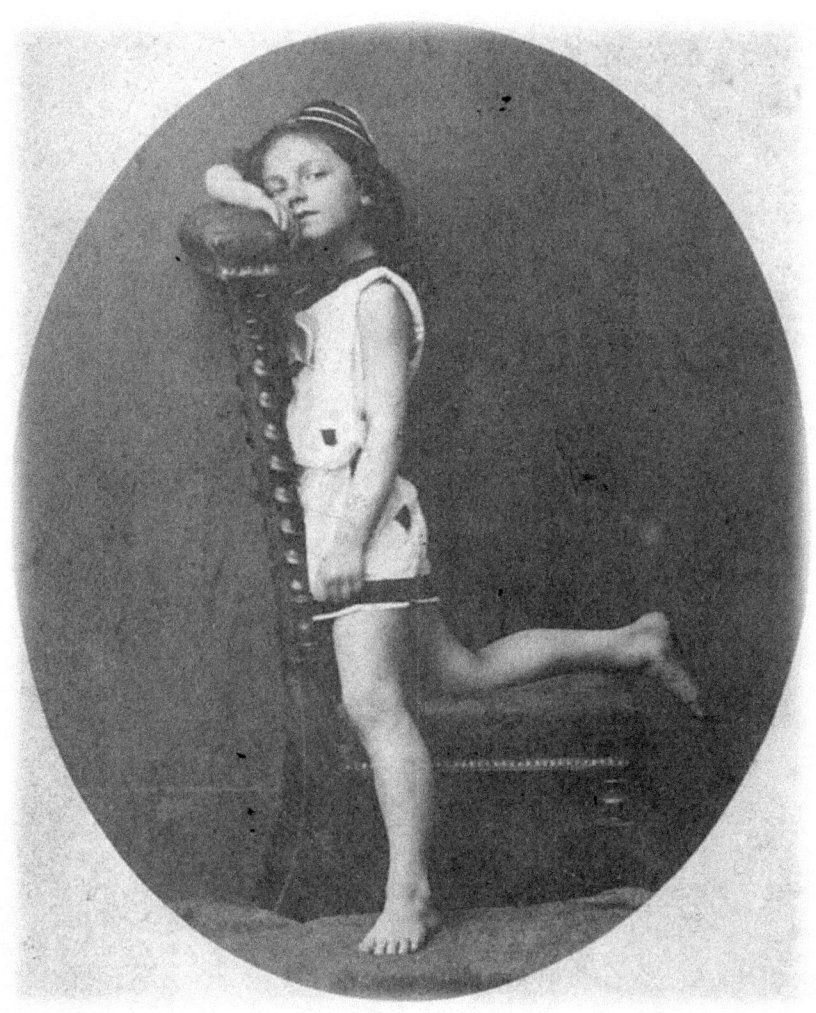

Evelyn Hatch, June 15, 1880

Evelyn Hatch, who he photographed nude as "Odalisque." recalls, "What I remember most about Mr. Dodgson was his kindness.... his aim was to give happiness and to make life richer... he was an ever-welcome guest."

The reclining photograph of Evelyn was included in Britain's Tate Gallery 2014 show called Exposed: The Victorian Nude.

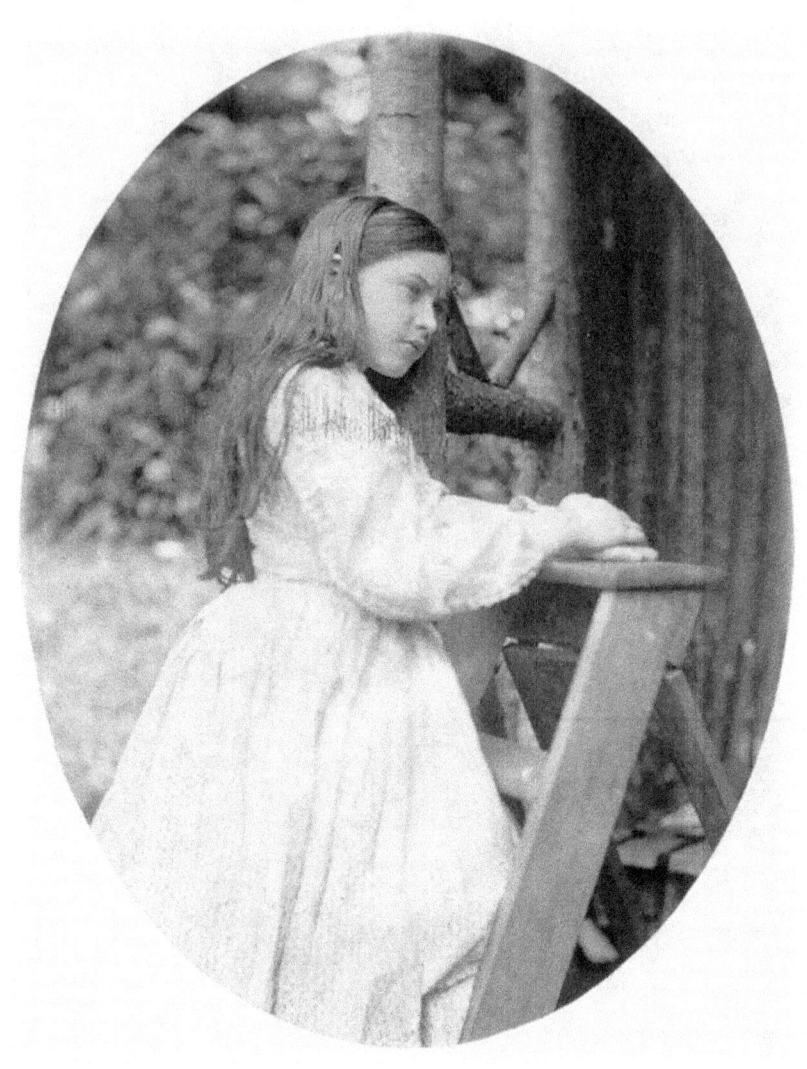

Dymphna Ellis, July 25, 1865

Daughter of the Rector of Cranbourne

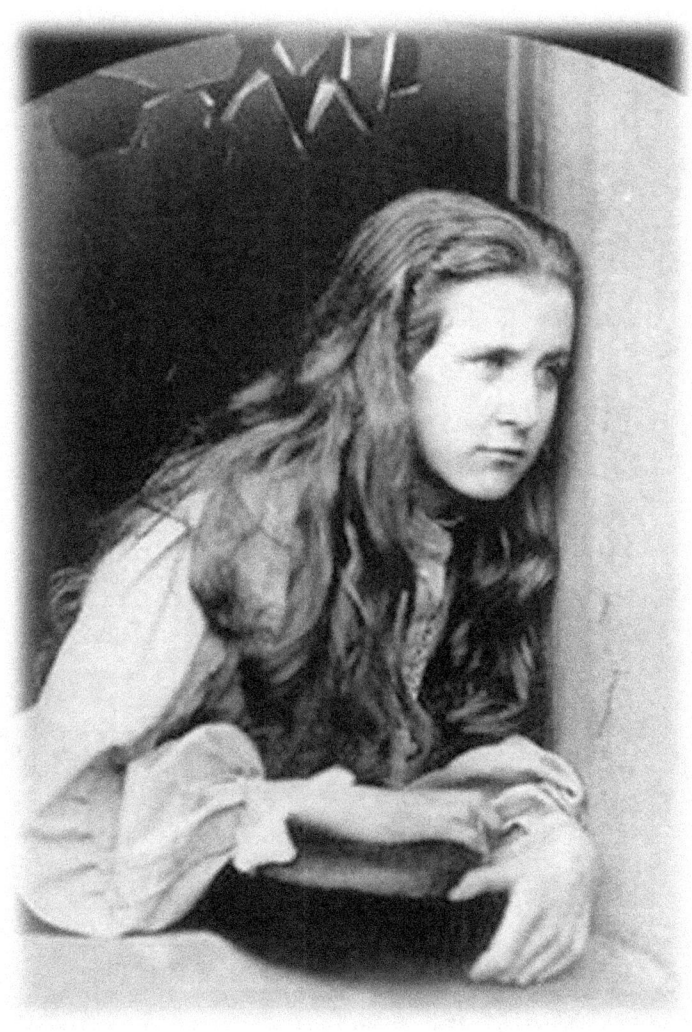

Dymphna Ellis

What is "F" before "Dymphna"? Is it Fatima, Fenella or Feodora? or is it (I hardly dare hope for so beautiful a name) Foscofornia?

- Letter from Carroll to Dymphna Ellis (3 Aug 1865)

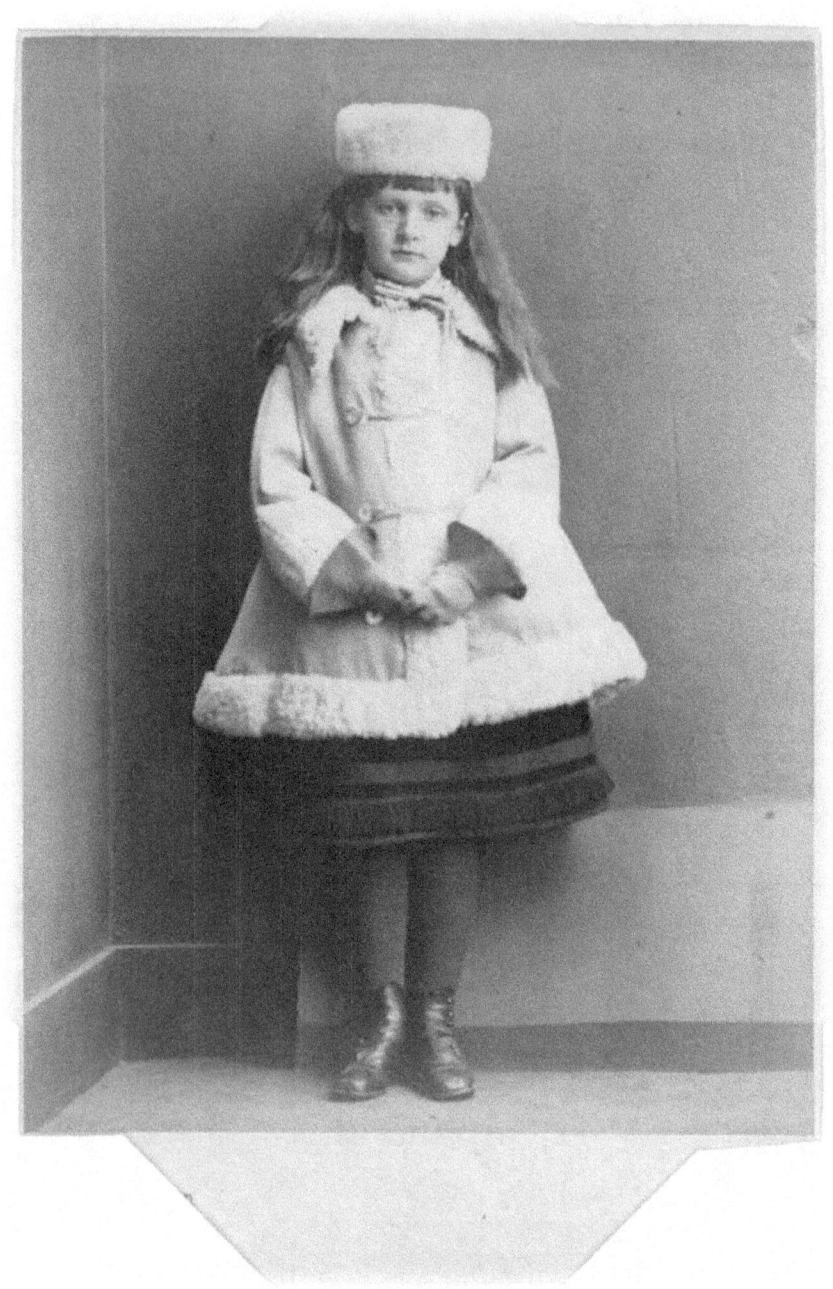

Xie Kitchin

Carroll's most photographed subject

Posing for the Rev. Charles L. Dodgson (1832–1898) for over a dozen years, Alexandra "Xie" Kitchin (1864–1925) grows up before our eyes through the series of portraits made of her during the 1860s and 1870s. Named after Princess (later Queen) Alexandra, who was a close friend of her mother, Xie (pronounced "Ecksy") was the daughter of a clerical colleague of Dodgson's at Christ Church College in Oxford. She began sitting for Dodgson's tableaux at the early age of four, and, by at least one historian's count, sat for him more than 50 times before she turned 16. Several other children—or "child-friends"—that Dodgson photographed were quickly bored with dressing up and sitting for long poses before the camera, but Xie participated well into her teens and is frequently referenced in the photographer's diaries.

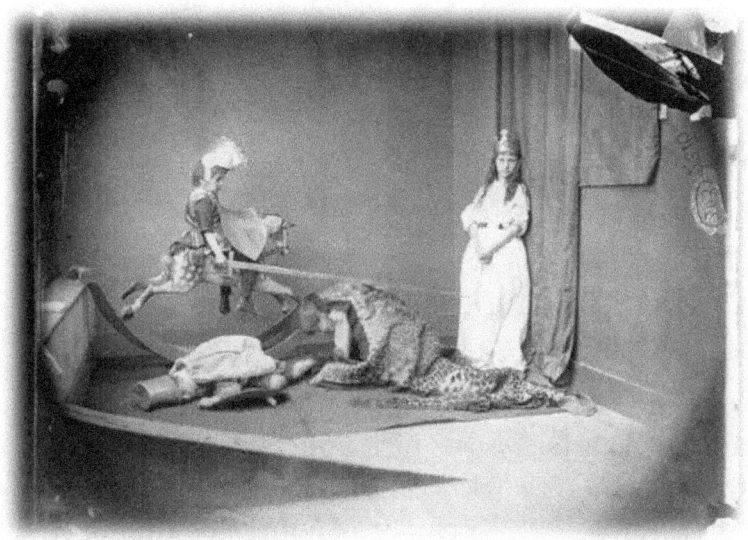

"St. George and the Dragon" 1875

Xie Kitchin and her brothers: Brook (on the rocking horse), Hugh (in leopard skin, as the dragon), and Herbert (a fallen would-be rescuer).

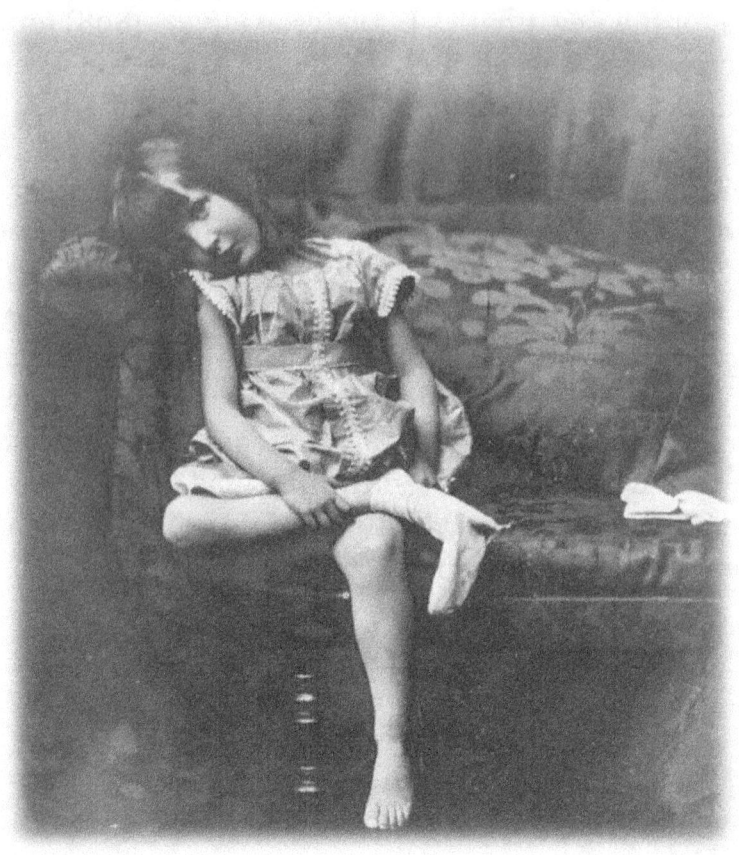

Xie, Badcock yard studio, 1869

Alexandra Kitchin, whose nickname was Xie (pronounced "Ecksy"). Carroll created a pun with her name, when he told her father, Rev. G. W. Kitchin, upon meeting him for the first time, how to achieve excellence from a photo: "All you have to do is to get a lens and put Xie before it."

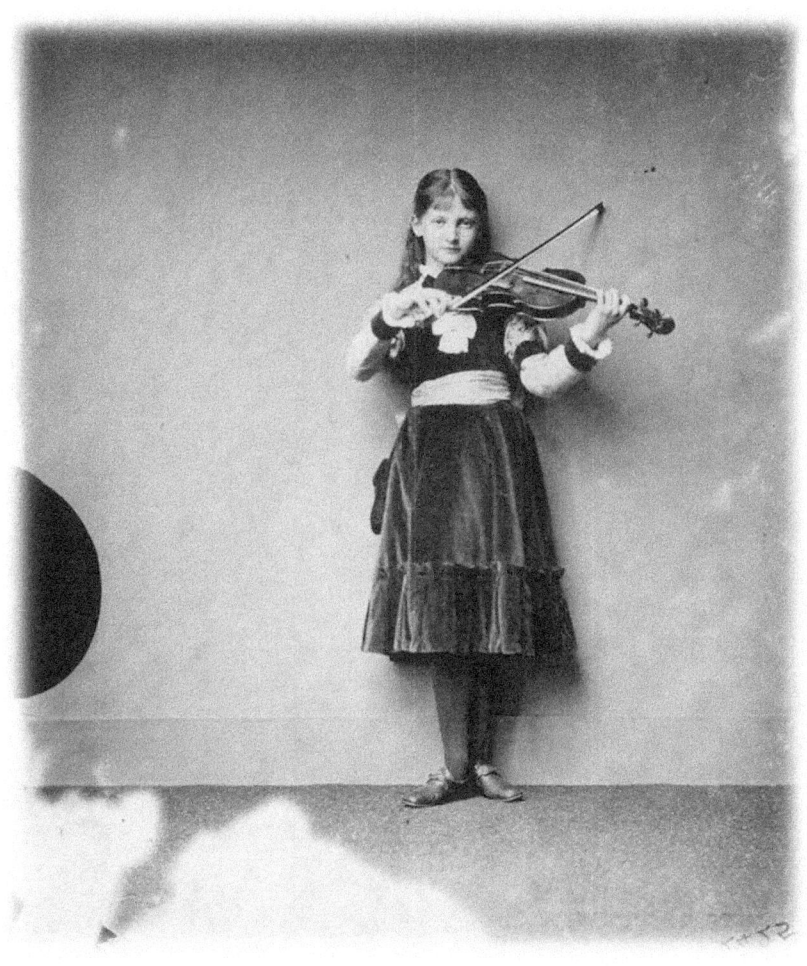

Xie Kitchin, "tuning", taken in Carroll's studio, July 1, 1876.

The violin wasn't just a prop, Xie really did play

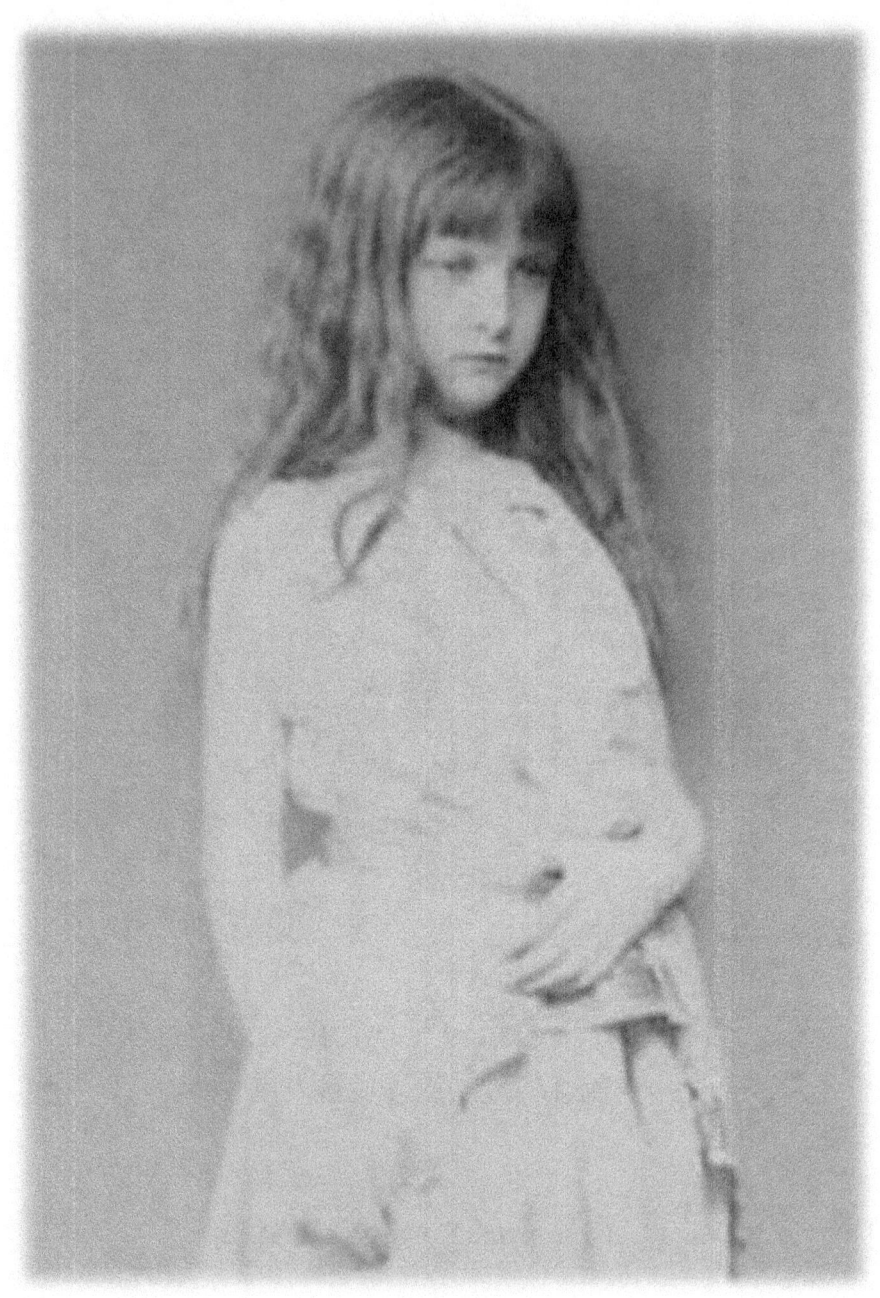

Xie Kitchin

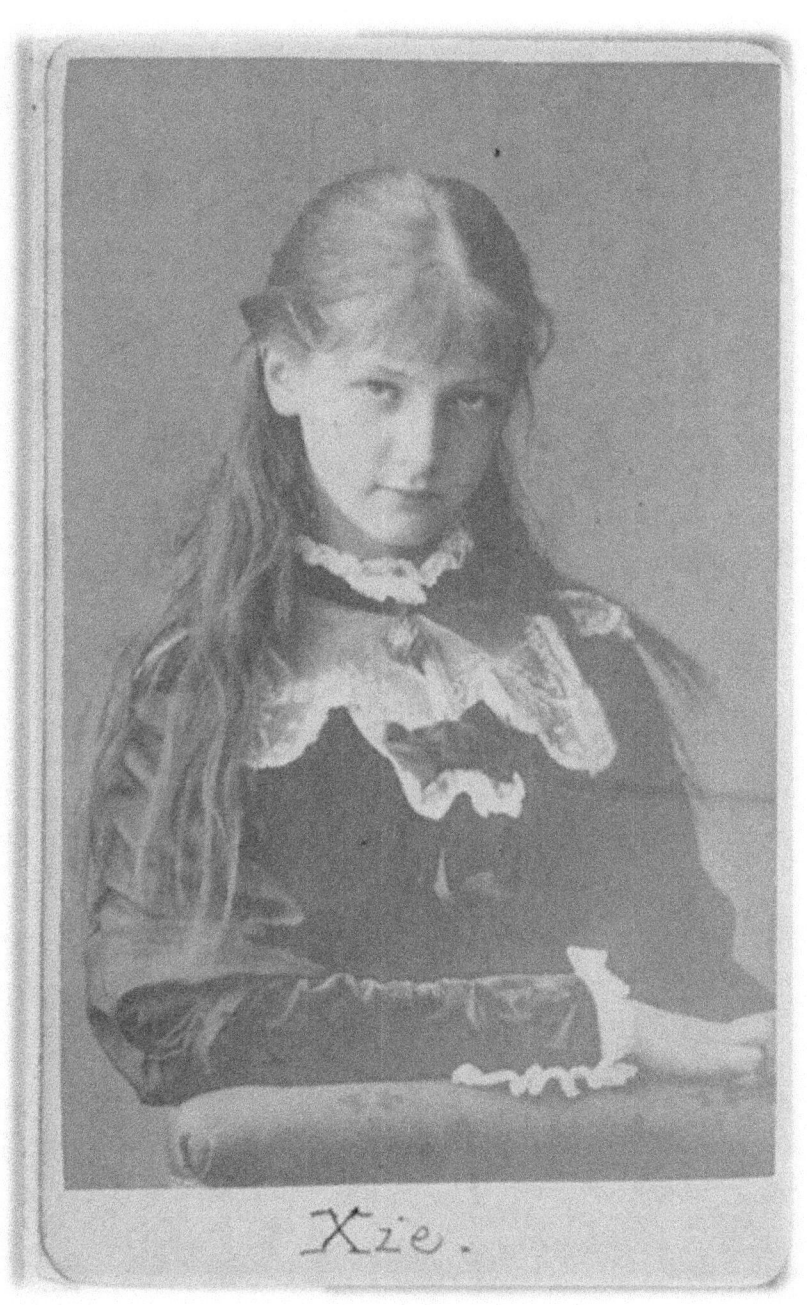

Xie Kitchin

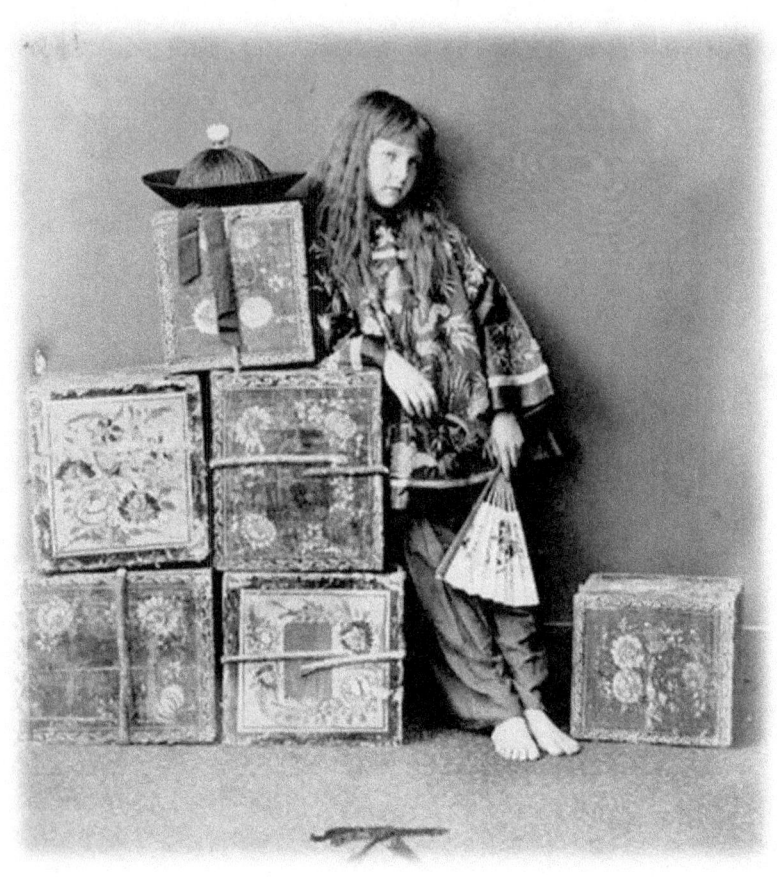

Xie Kitchin

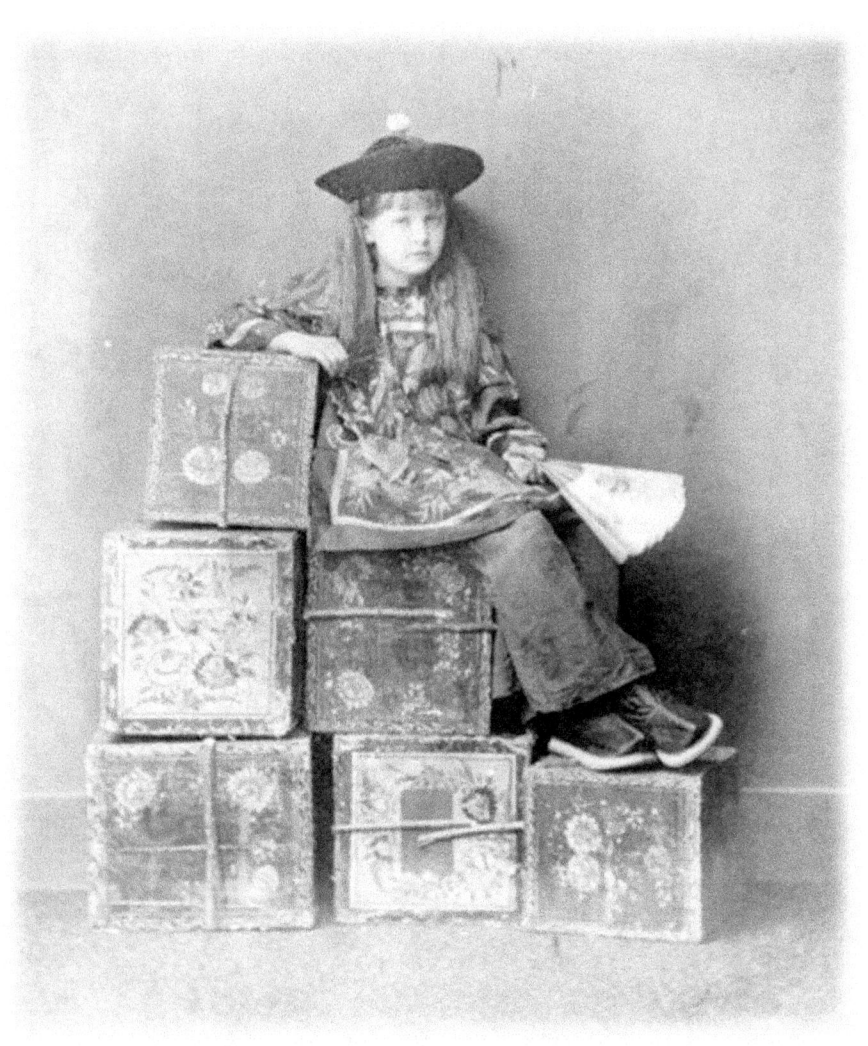

Xie Kitchin

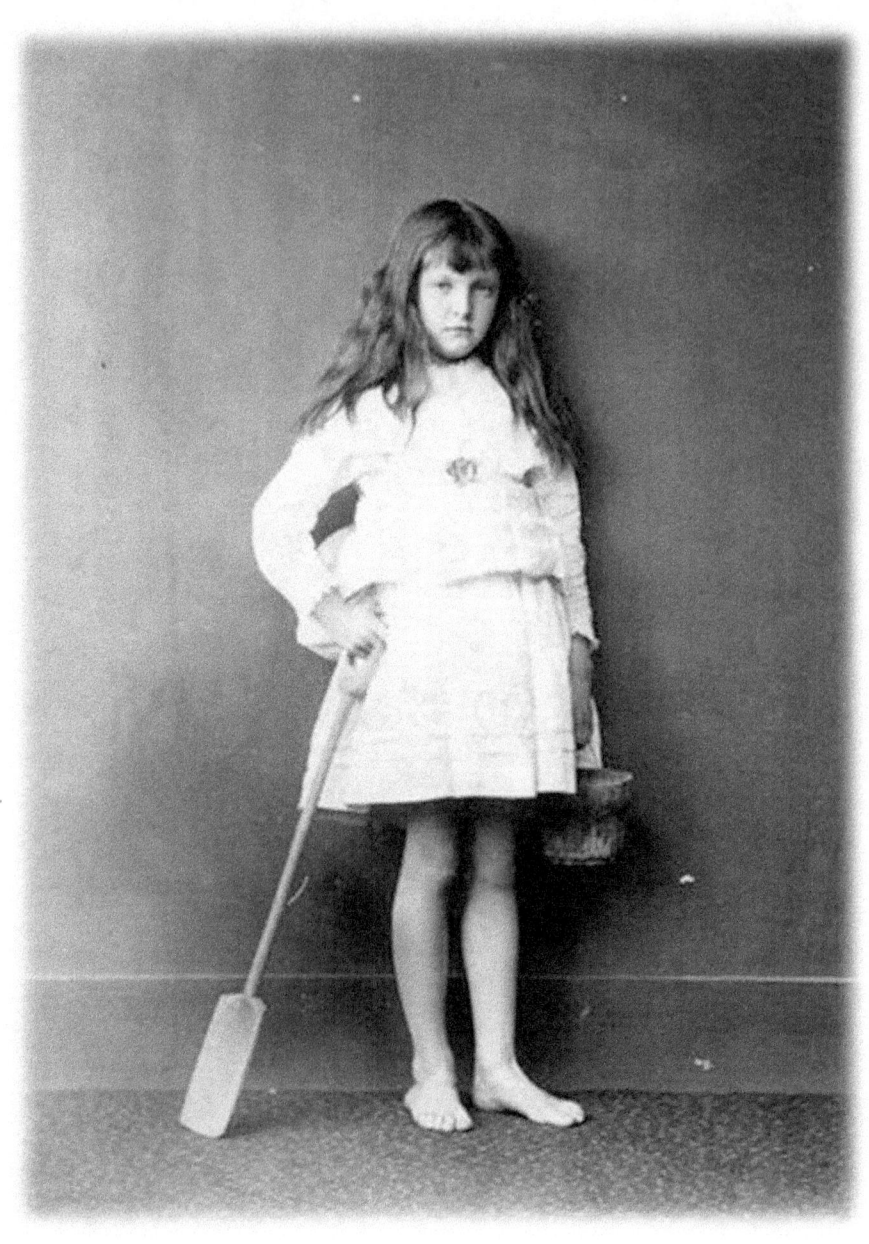

Xie Kitchin

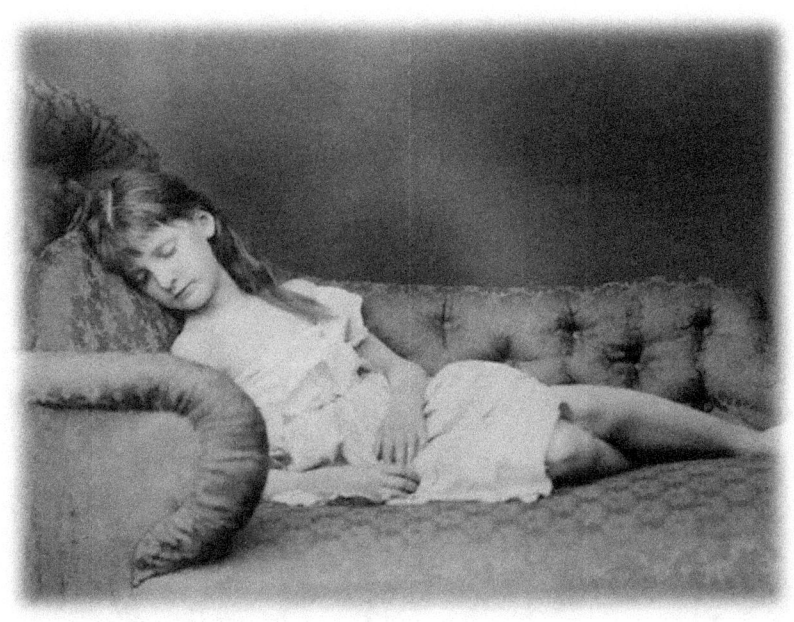

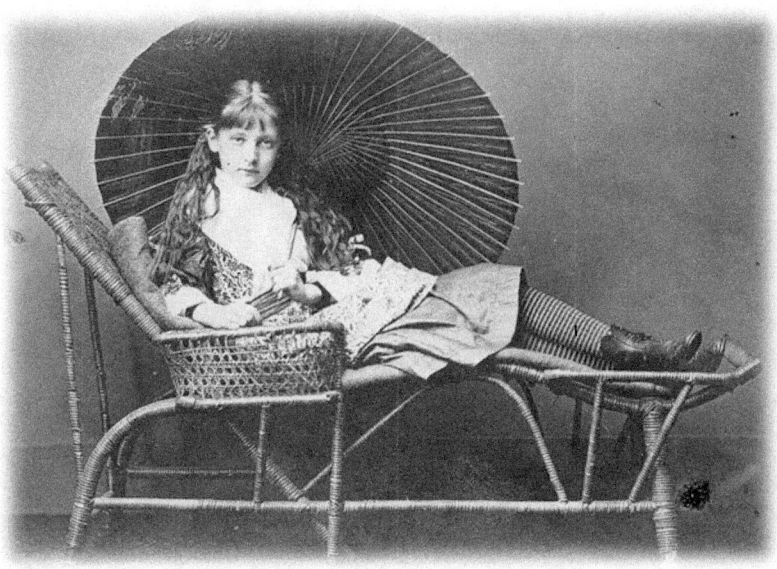

Xie Kitchin

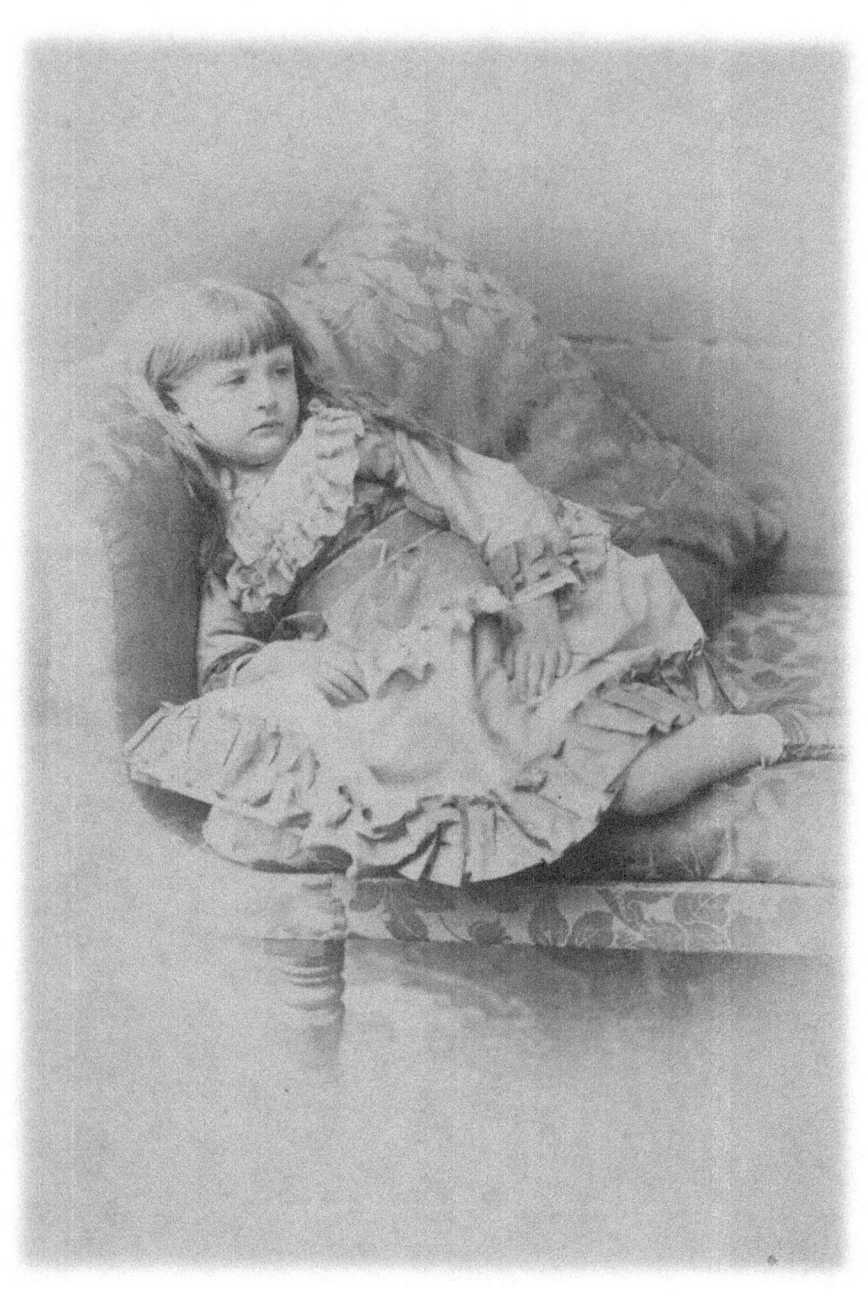

Xie Kitchin

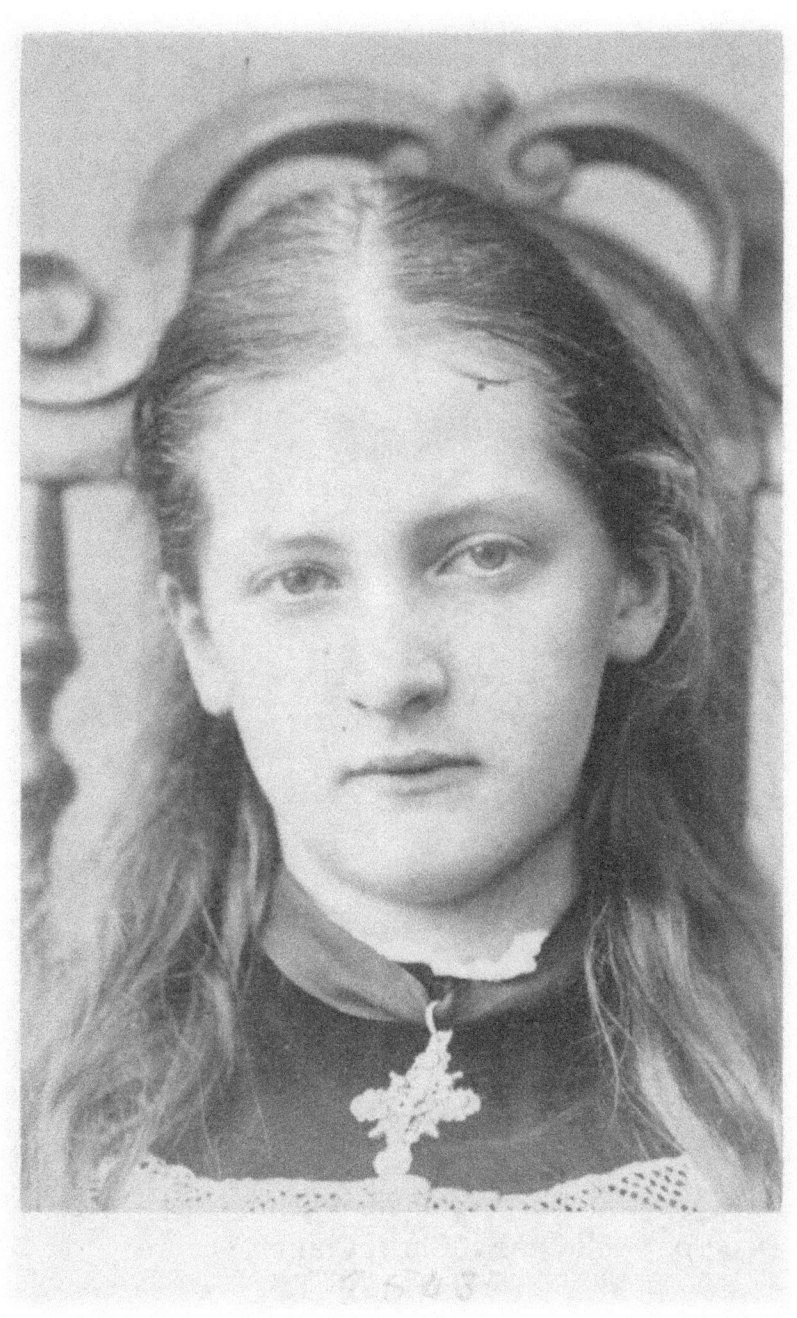

Xie Kitchin

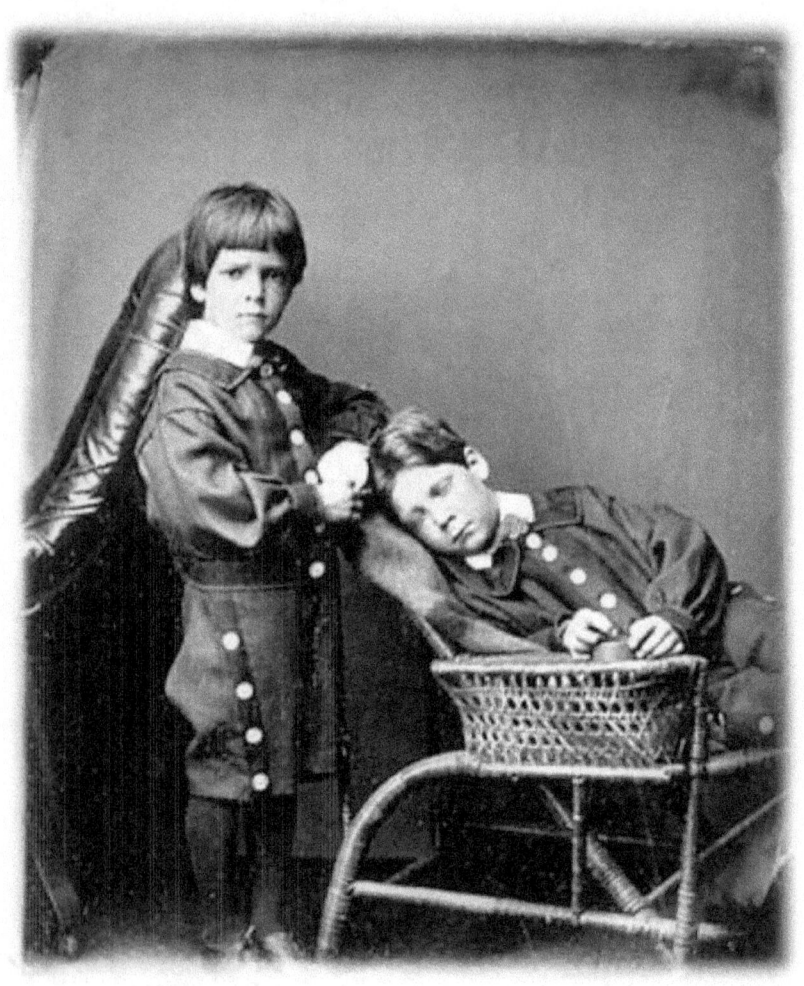

The brothers of 'Xie' Kitchin

Brook and Hugh 1876

The sons of Rev. George William Kitchin (1827–1912), who was Dodgson's colleague at Christ Church, Oxford

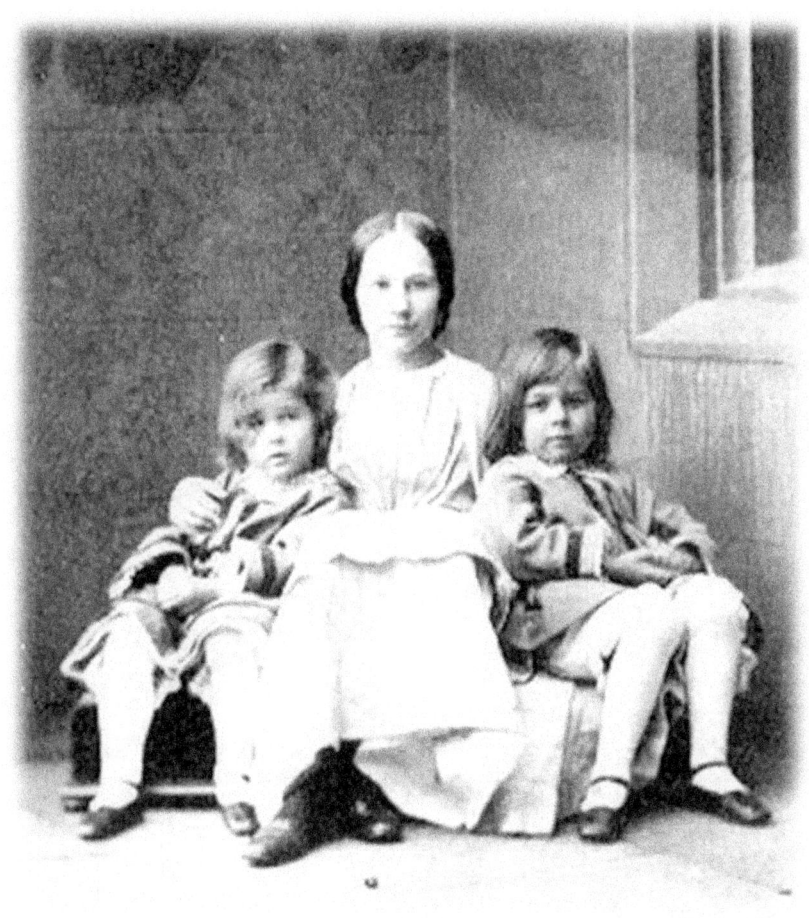

Hallam and Lionel Tennyson

With Julia Marshall 1857

The sons of Alfred Tennyson, 1st Baron Tennyson, FRS was Poet Laureate of Great Britain and Ireland during much of Queen Victoria's reign.

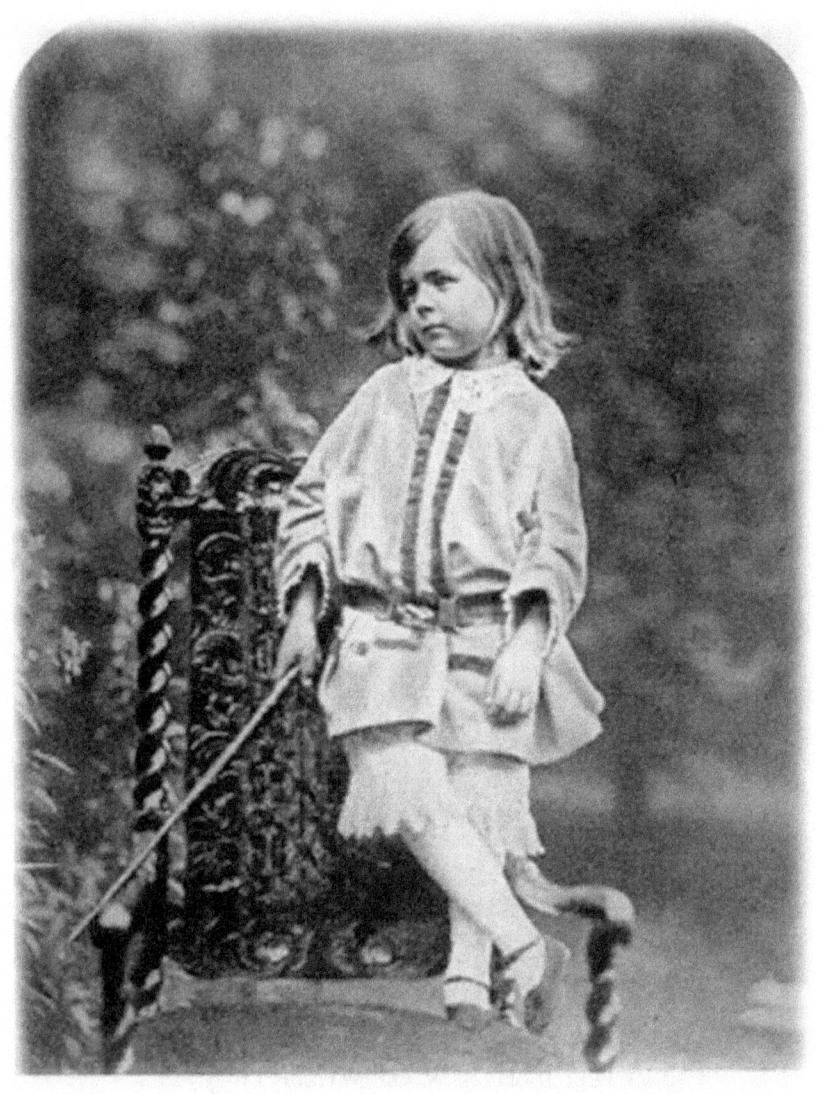

Hallam Tennyson (b.1852-1928)

He was the oldest son of the poet **Alfred, Lord Tennyson**

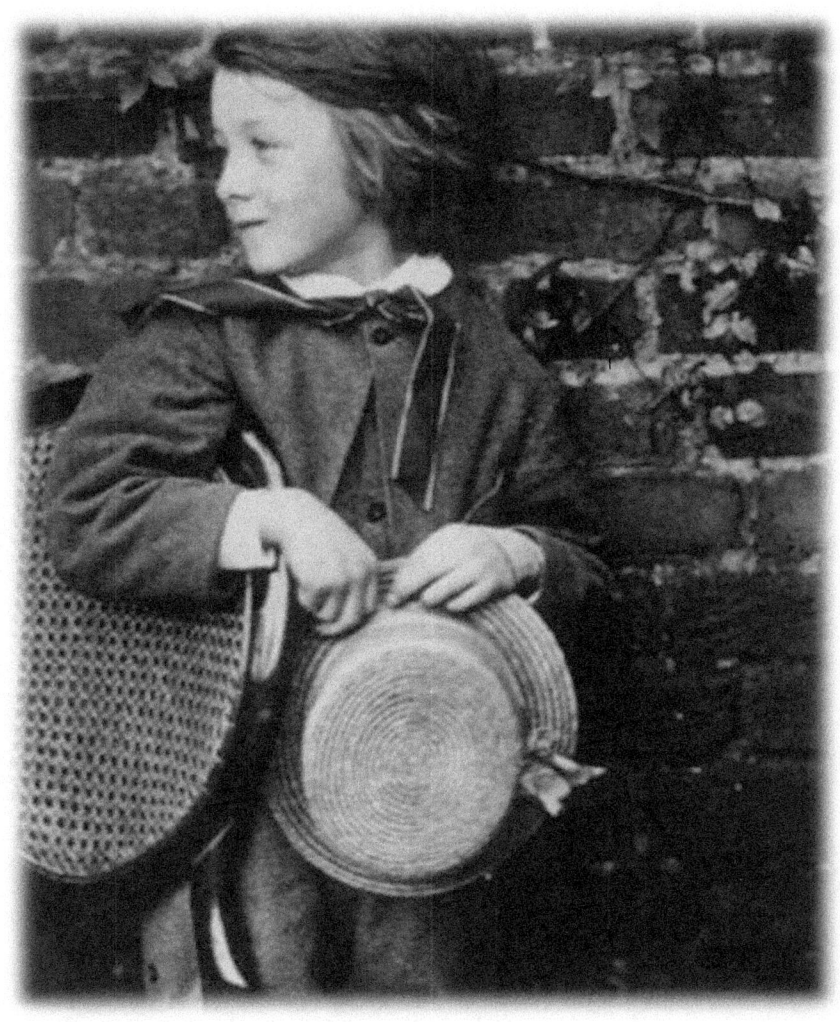

Arthur Foord Hughes (b.1856- 1914)

The son of the **Pre-Raphaelite** painter Arthur Hughes, and his wife and former model, Tryphena Foord

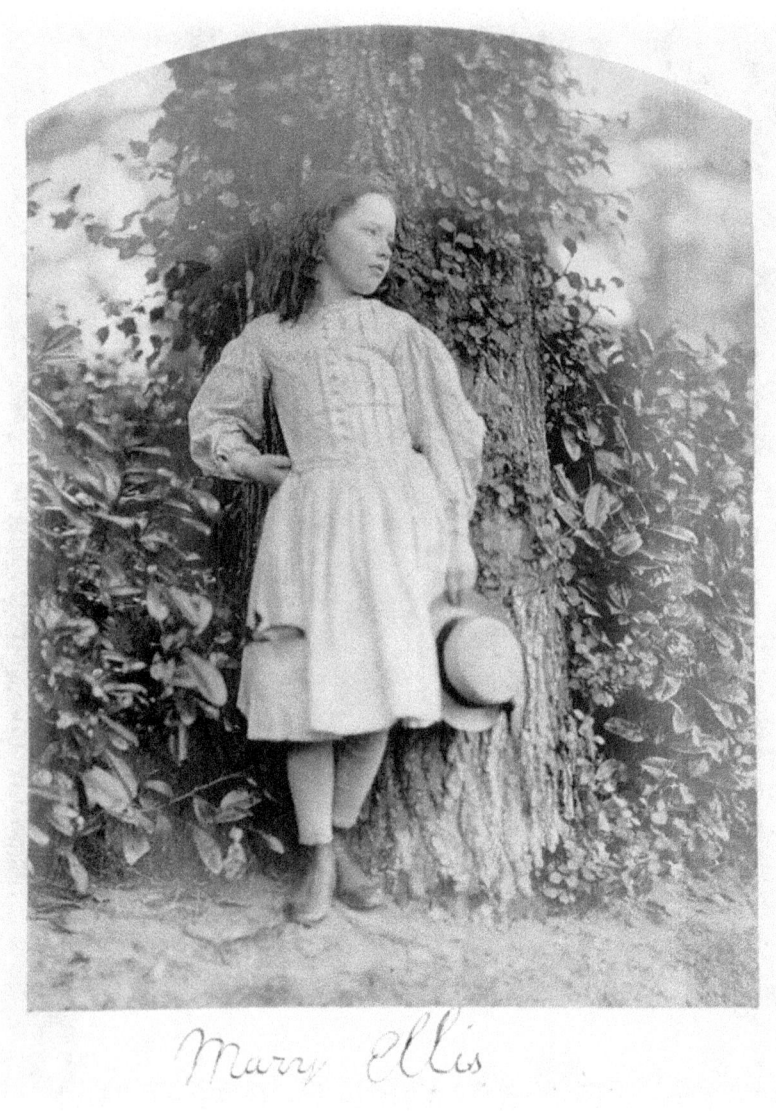

Mary Ellis (aged 9), July 26 or 27, 1865

Carroll took a number of pictures of Mary and her three sisters at that time.

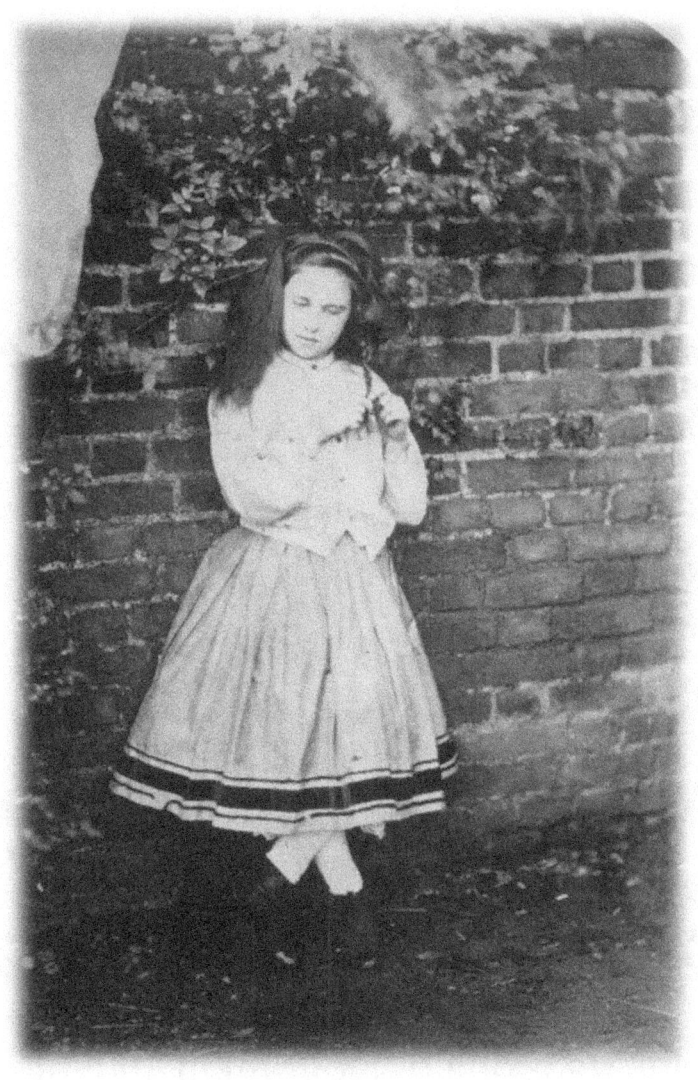

Mary MacDonald

My room is very easy to find when you get here, and as for *distance*, you know - why, Oxford is as near to London as London is to Oxford. If your geography-book doesn't tell you *that*, it must be a wretched affair.

- Letter to Mary MacDonald (22 January 1866)

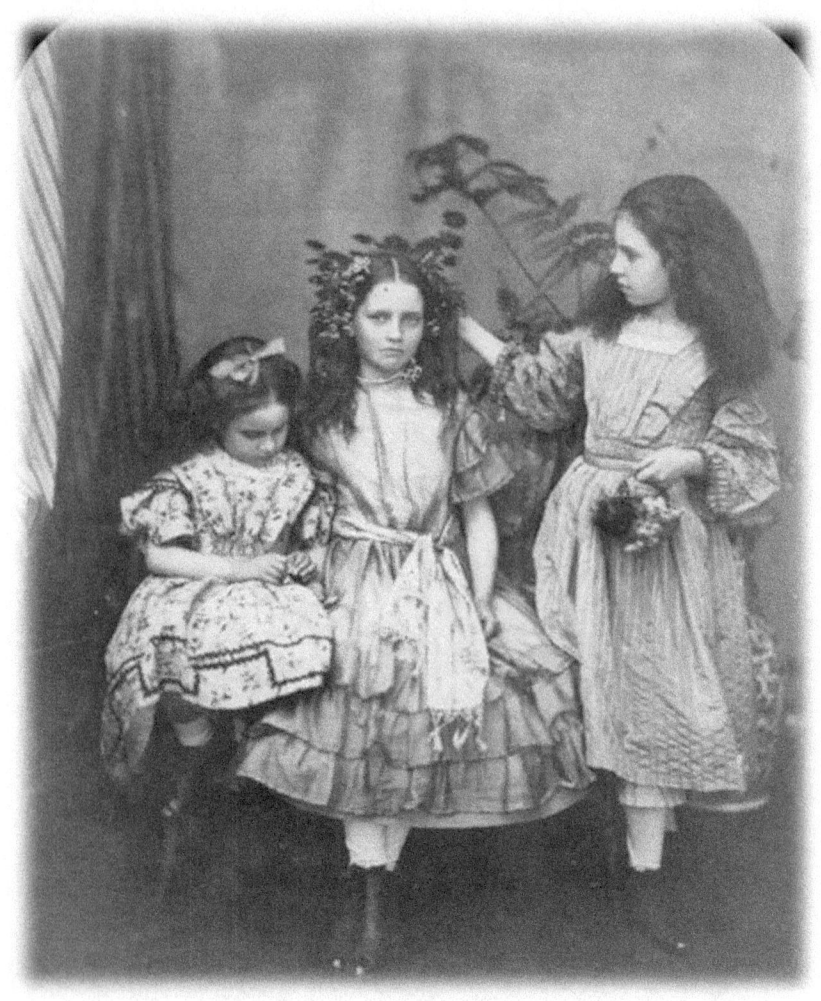

Irene MacDonald, Flo Rankin and Mary MacDonald

Irene and Mary MacDonald were two of the five children of Scottish novelist and poet George MacDonald. Carroll was a friend of the family, and the children affectionately called him "Uncle." It was the MacDonalds to whom he read the manuscript of The Adventures of Alice and who urged him to publish the work. This photograph, which includes the children's friend Flo Rankin standing in the middle, was produced during the photographer's stay at Elm Lodge in Hampstead the week of July 25, 1863.

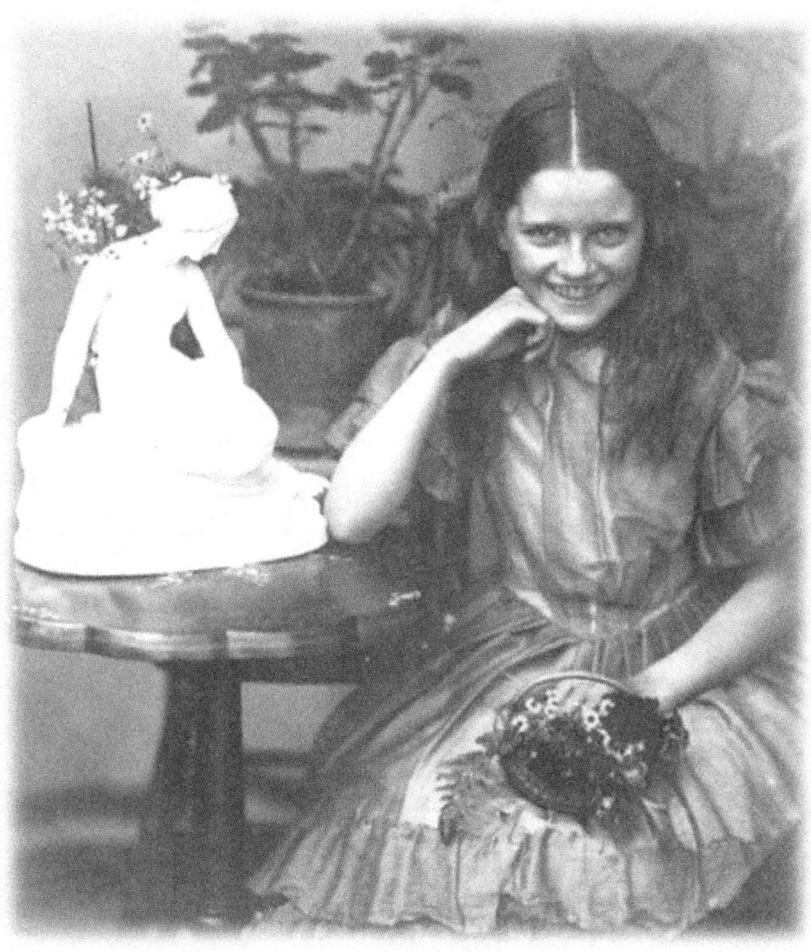

Flo Rankin

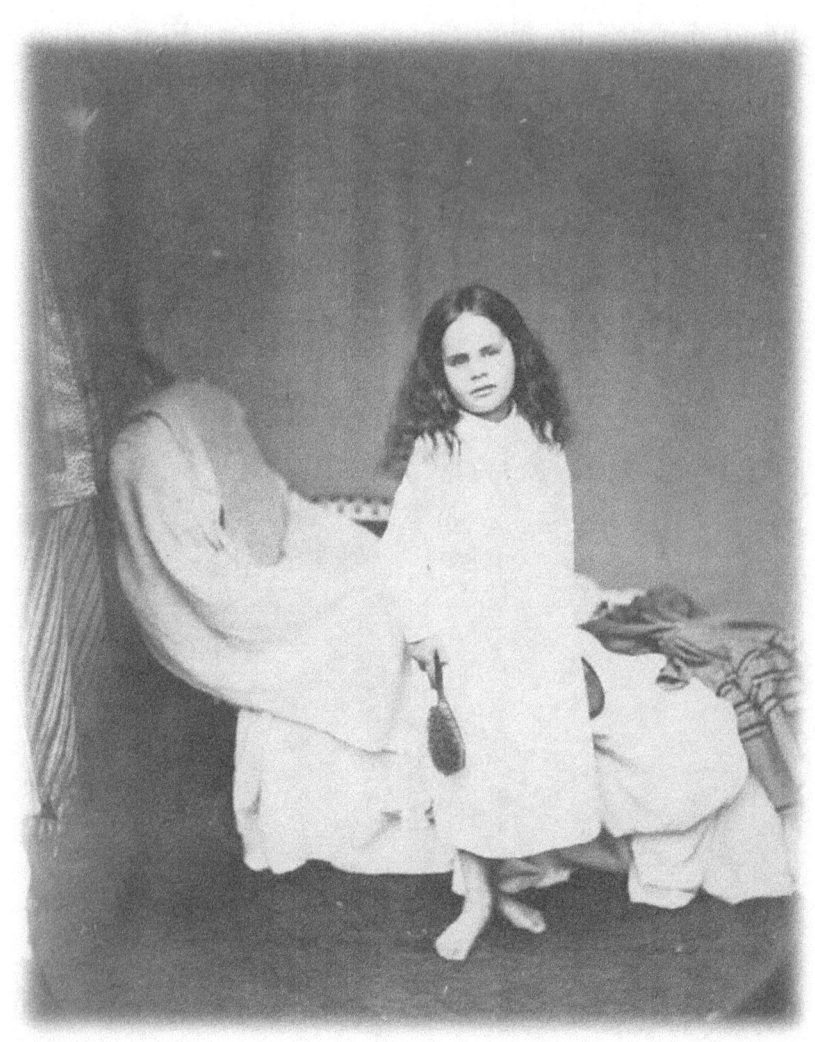

Irene MacDonald

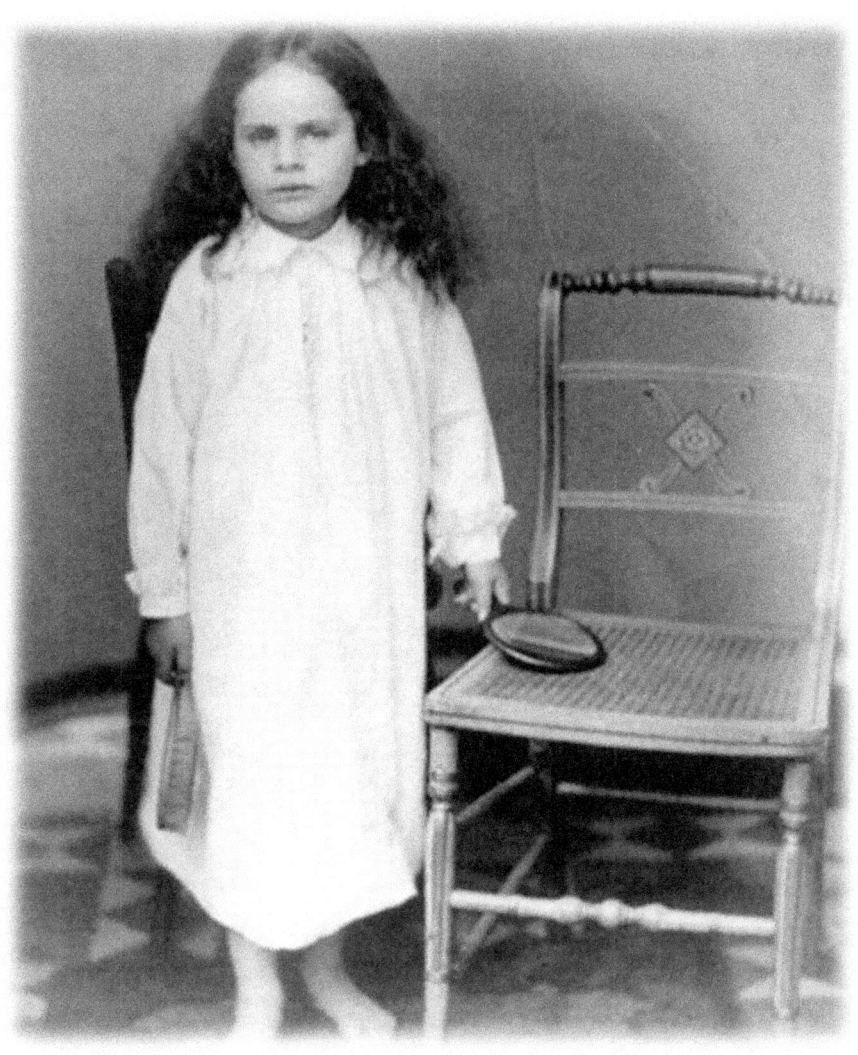

Irene MacDonald

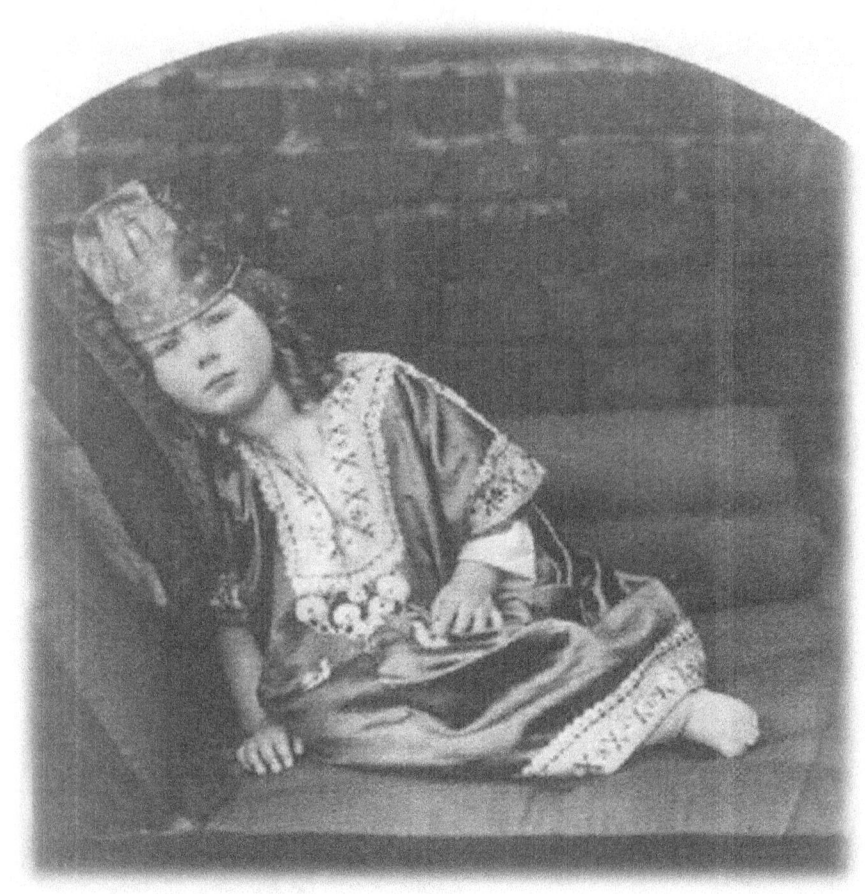

Agnes Hughes 1863

My dear Agnes,

You lazy thing! What? I'm to divide the kisses myself, am I? Indeed, I won't take the trouble to do anything of the sort!

CARROLL 1871

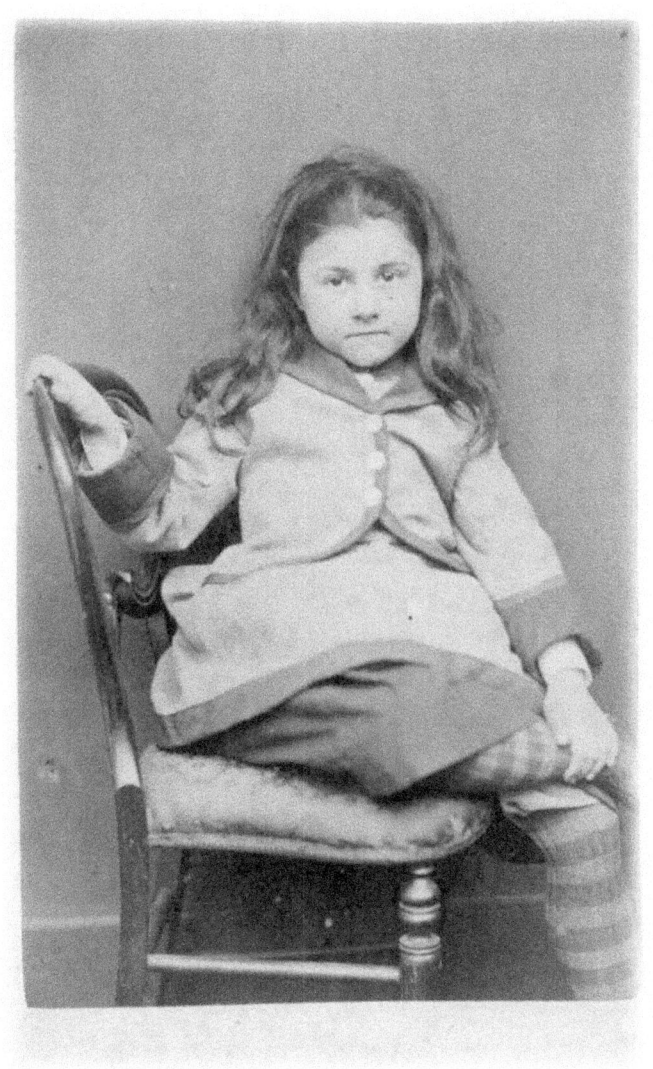

Beatrice "Birdie" Hatch (1866-1947)

One of Carroll's favourite models

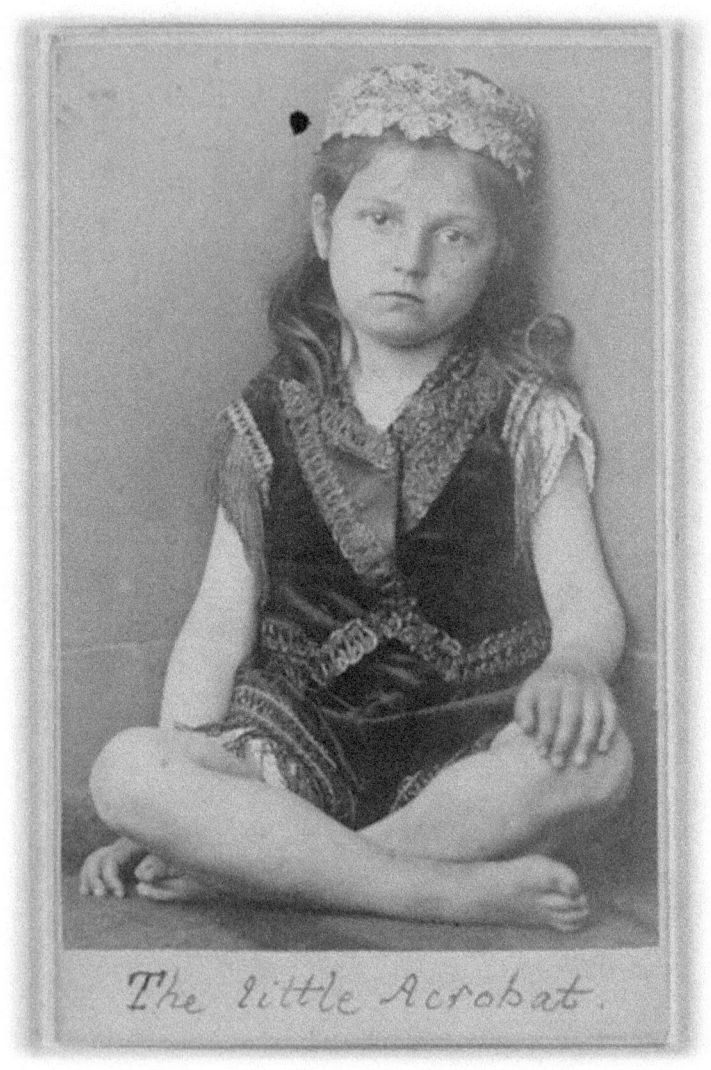

Beatrix Hatch

Beatrice Sheward Hatch (1866 – 20 December 1947) was an Englishwoman and **muse** of Charles Lutwidge Dodgson, She was one of a select few children that Dodgson photographed nude, therefore making Hatch the subject of much contemporary study and speculation. Photographs of Hatch still inspire artistic work in contemporary times.

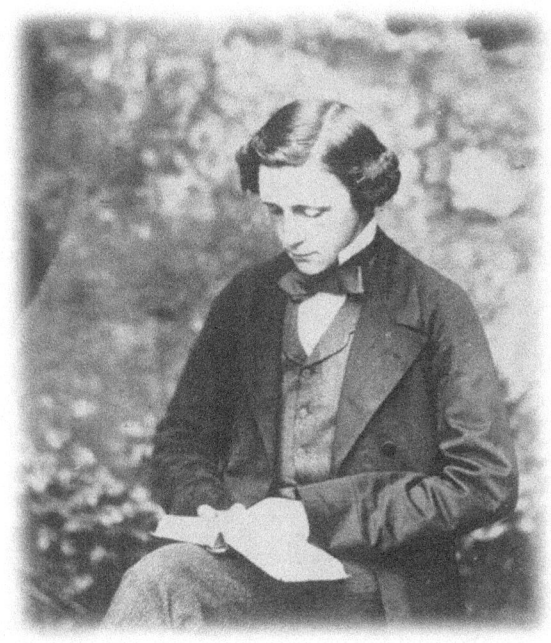

Carroll wrote a long letter (May 26, 1879) to Mrs. Mayhew asking for permission to photograph her younger daughters Ethel and Janet in the nude. After several correspondences, Mrs. Mayhew insisted that she be present at the photo sessions as a chaperon. Carroll wrote: "But the fact I have so unfortunately learnt, that you consider your presence essential, which is the same as saying 'I cannot trust you,' has taken away all the pleasure I could have in doing any such pictures, and most of my desire to photograph them again in any way. It is not pleasant to know one is not trusted."

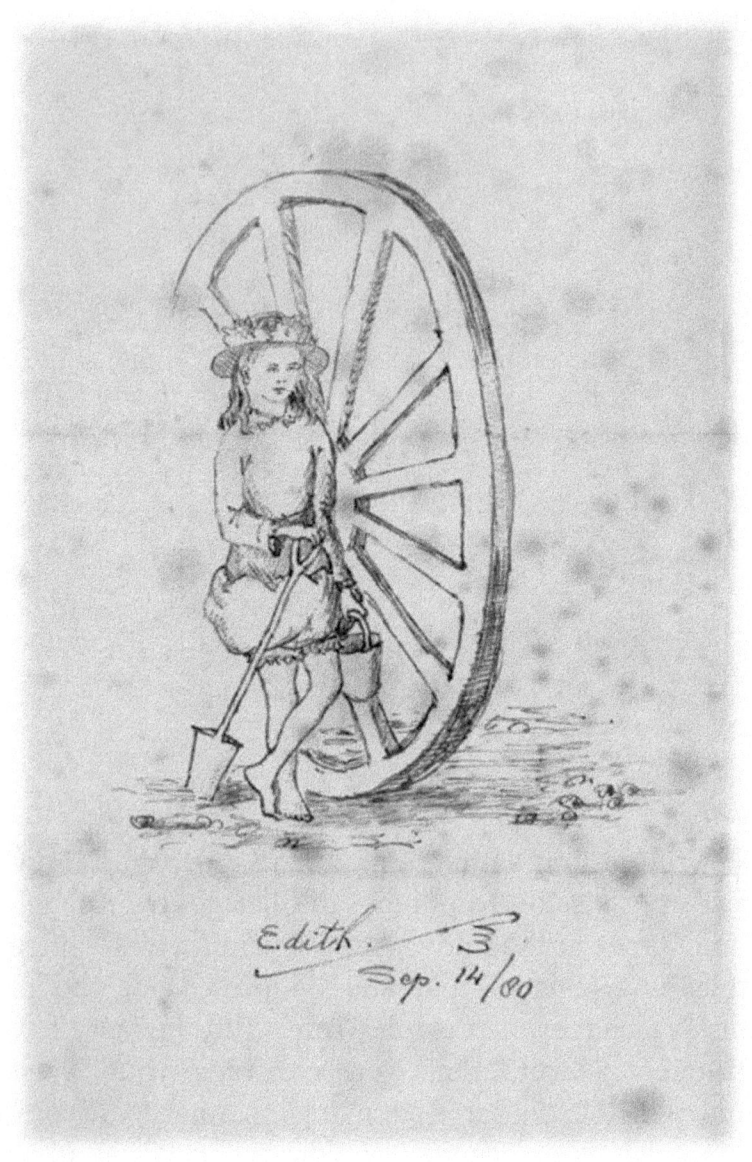

Carroll's drawing of Edith Blakemore, at Eastbourne, September 14, 1880

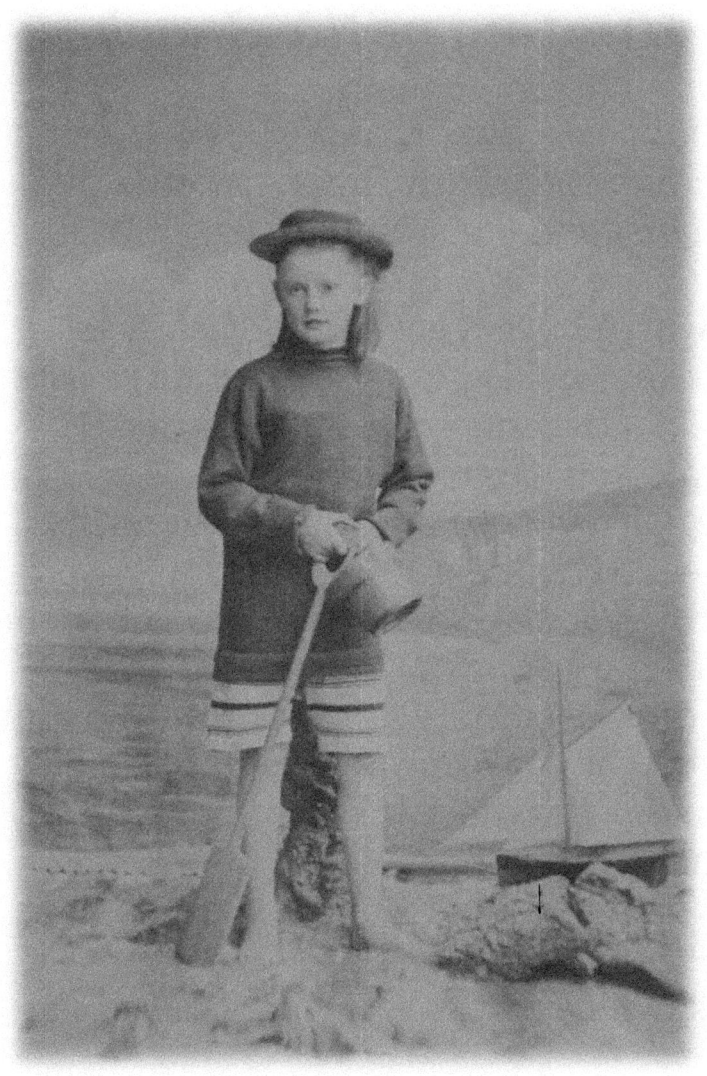

Gertrude Chataway

Carroll first became friends with Gertrude in 1875, when she was aged nine and he was forty-three, while on holiday at the English seaside resort of Sandown. It was Gertrude who inspired his great nonsense mock-epic *The Hunting of the Snark* (1876), and the book is dedicated to her, and opens with a poem that uses her name as a double acrostic.

The Hunting of the Snark

*Inscribed to a dear Child:
in memory of golden summer hours
and whispers of a summer sea.*

Girt with a boyish garb for boyish task,
Eager she wields her spade: yet loves as well
Rest on a friendly knee, intent to ask
The tale he loves to tell.
Rude spirits of the seething outer strife,
Unmeet to read her pure and simple spright,
Deem, if you list, such hours a waste of life,
Empty of all delight!
Chat on, sweet Maid, and rescue from annoy
Hearts that by wiser talk are unbeguiled.
Ah, happy he who owns that tenderest joy,
The heart-love of a child!
Away, fond thoughts, and vex my soul no more!
Work claims my wakeful nights, my busy days—
Albeit bright memories of that sunlit shore
Yet haunt my dreaming gaze!

LEWIS CARROLL

1876

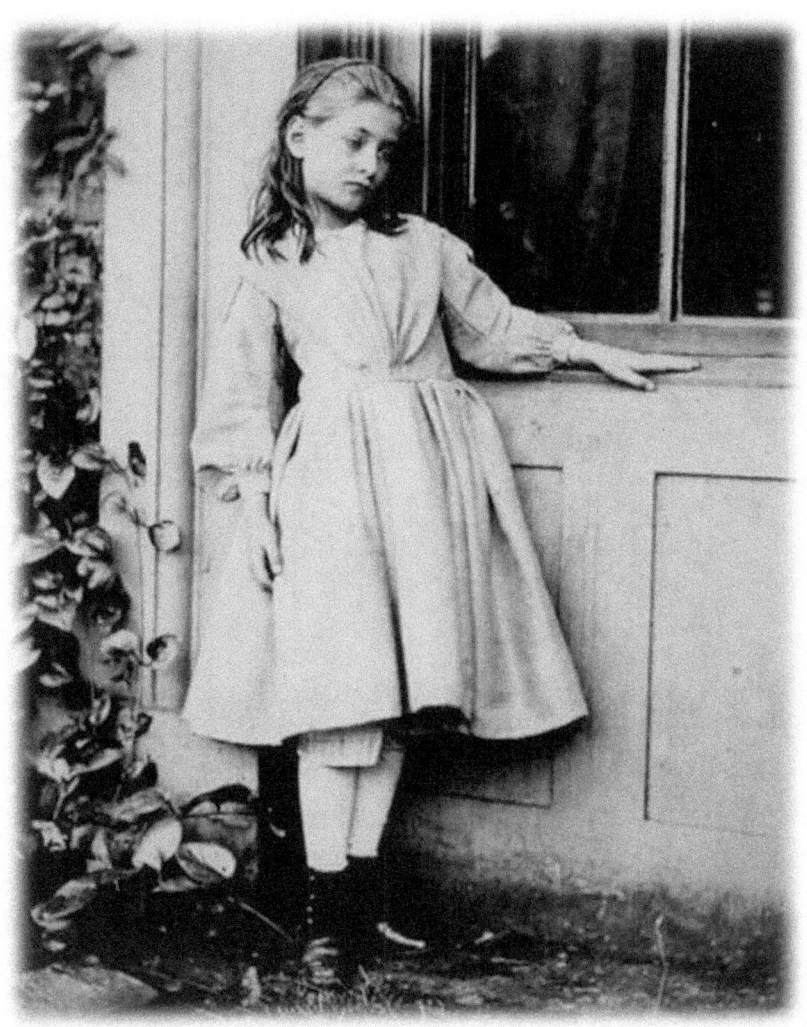

Gertrude Chataway

Gertrude Chataway (1866–1951) was the most important child-friend in the life of the author Lewis Carroll, after Alice Liddell.

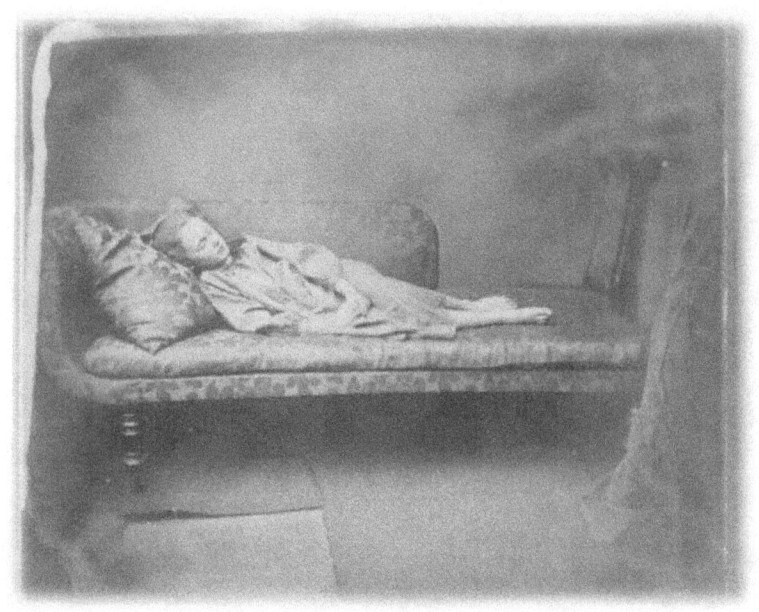

Gertrude Chataway

One of his favourite child friends, Gertrude Chataway, to her mother in the post script to a letter written June 28, 1876:

"If you should decide on sending over Gertrude and not coming yourself, would you kindly let me know what is the minimum amount of dress in which you are willing to have her taken?" He assured her that he rarely had a chance to photograph "so well-formed a subject for art."

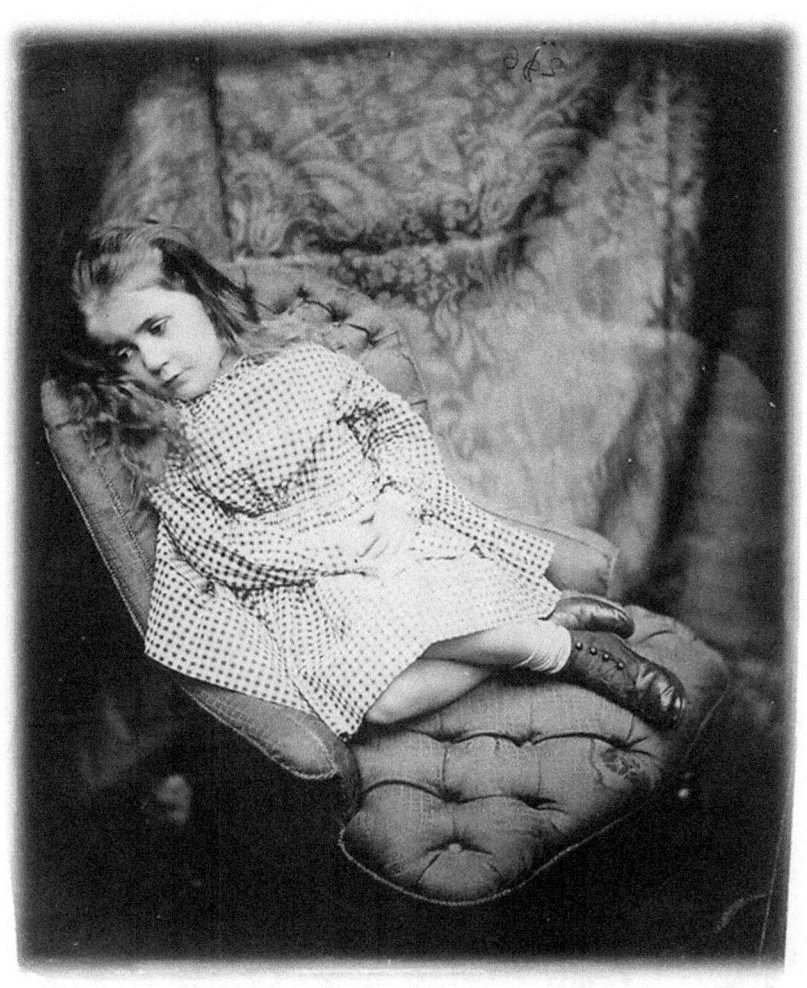

Margaret Frances Langton

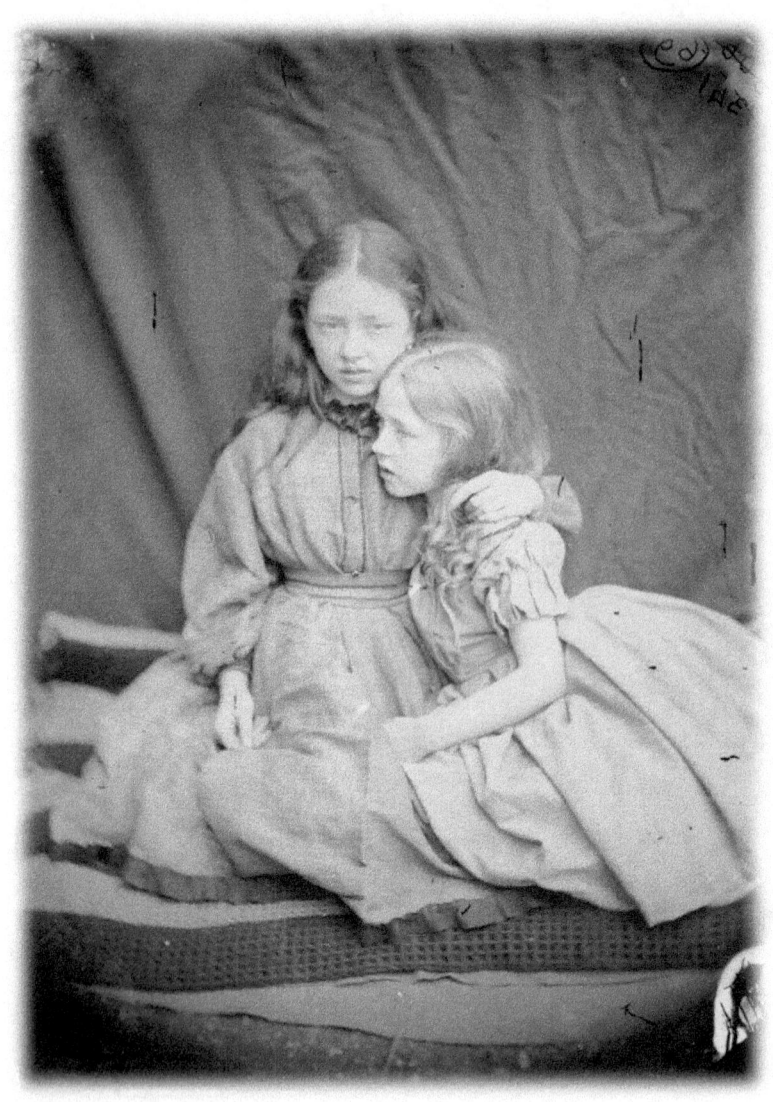

Marion and Florence Terry 1865

"Polly and Flo"; Marion and Florence Terry, younger sisters of actress Ellen Terry

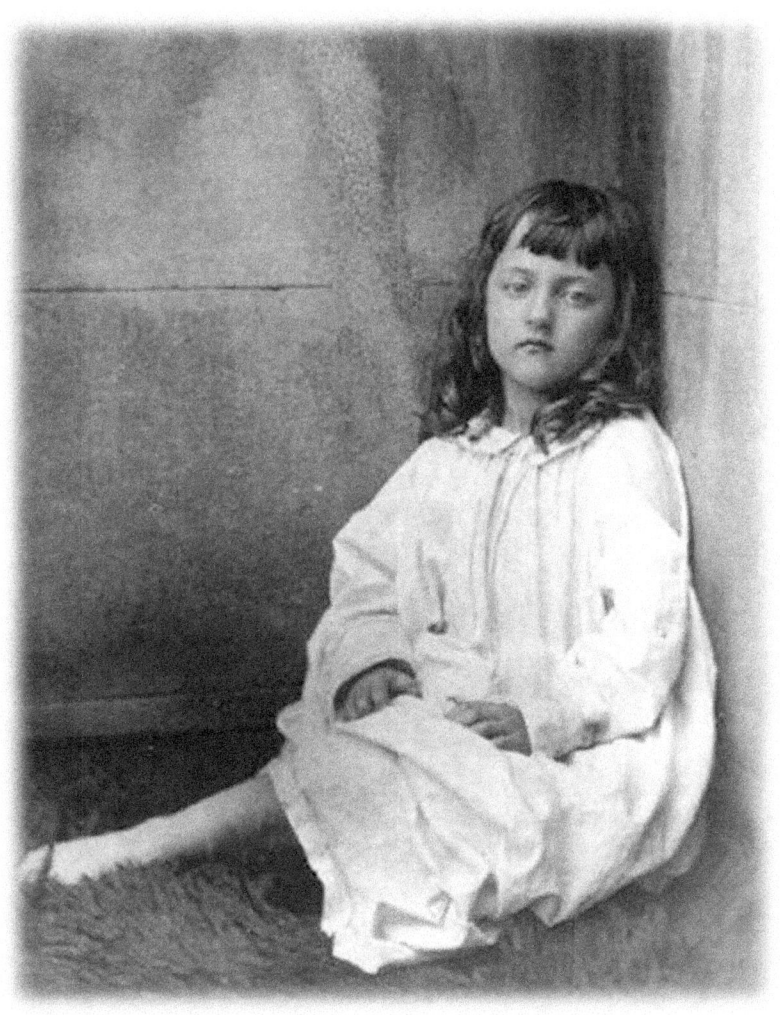

Mary Millais

Mary Millais, daughter of painter John Everett Millais, one of the founding members of the Pre-Raphaelite Brotherhood; taken July 21, 1865 at 7 Cromwell Place, London

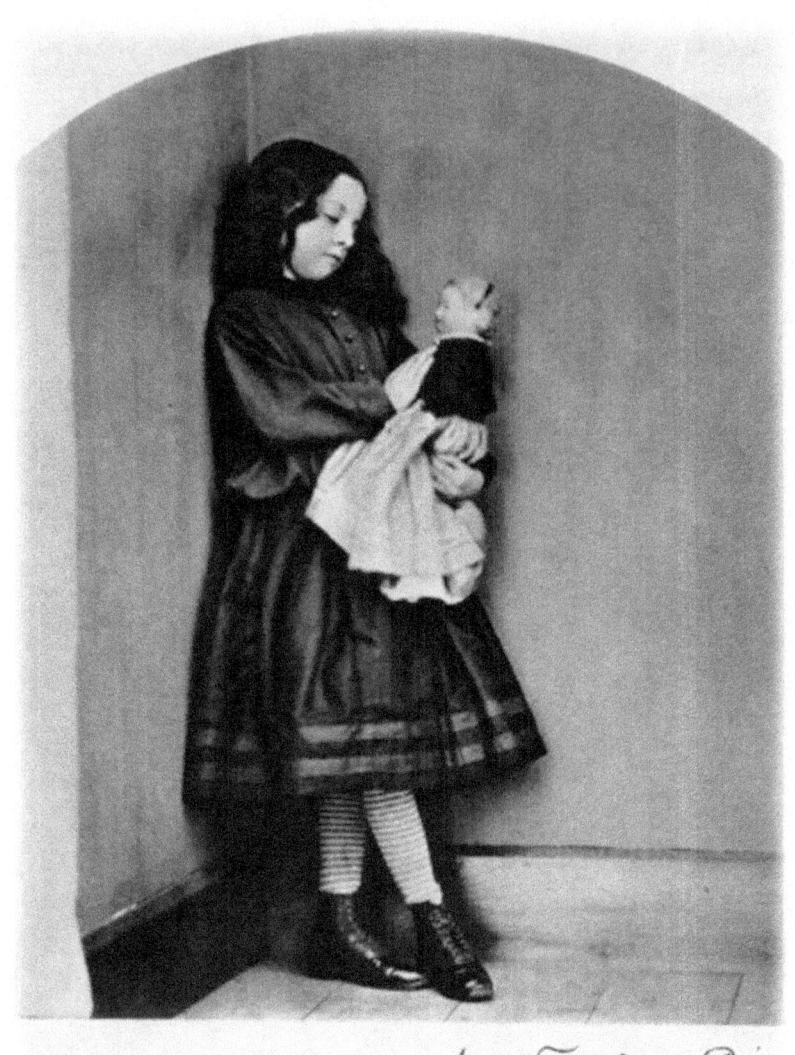

Agnes Florence Price

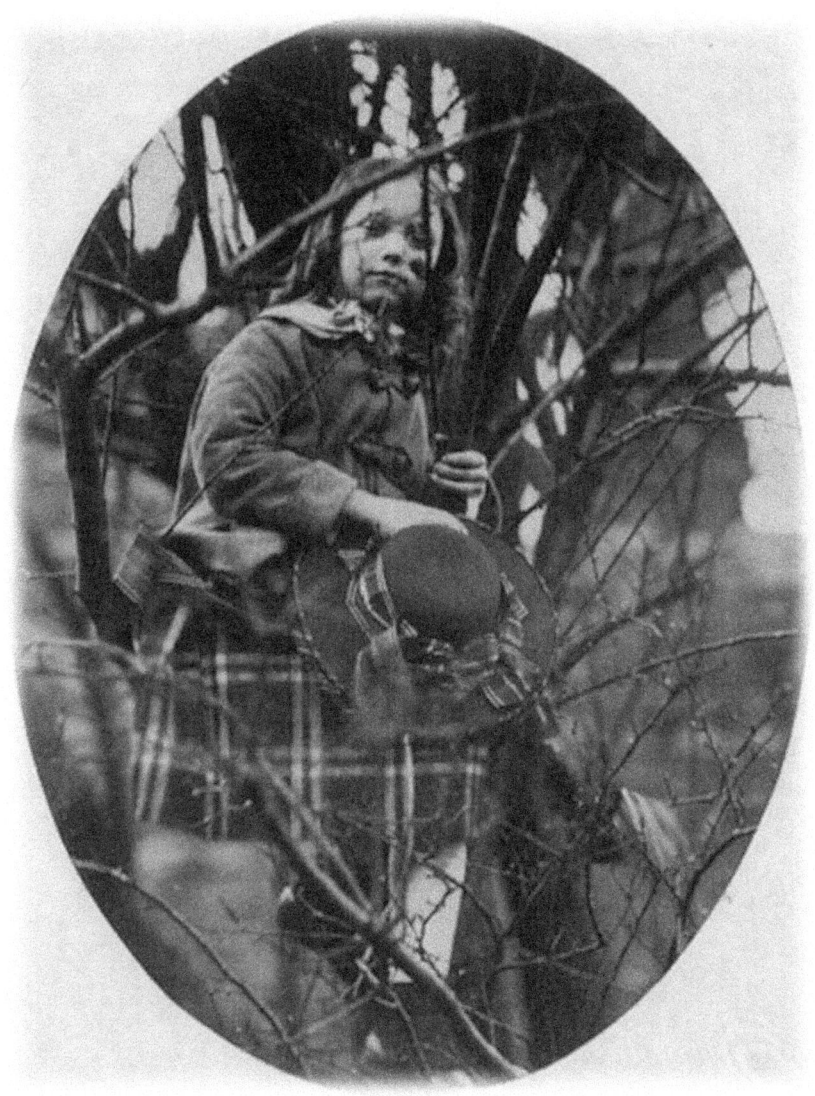

Kathleen Tidy

Carroll at his best: This unusual portrait, of Kathleen Tidy, was taken on her seventh birthday, April 1, 1858. She was born in Ireland, but was living with her grandmother in Littlethorp, Yorkshire, near Ripon, where this picture was taken

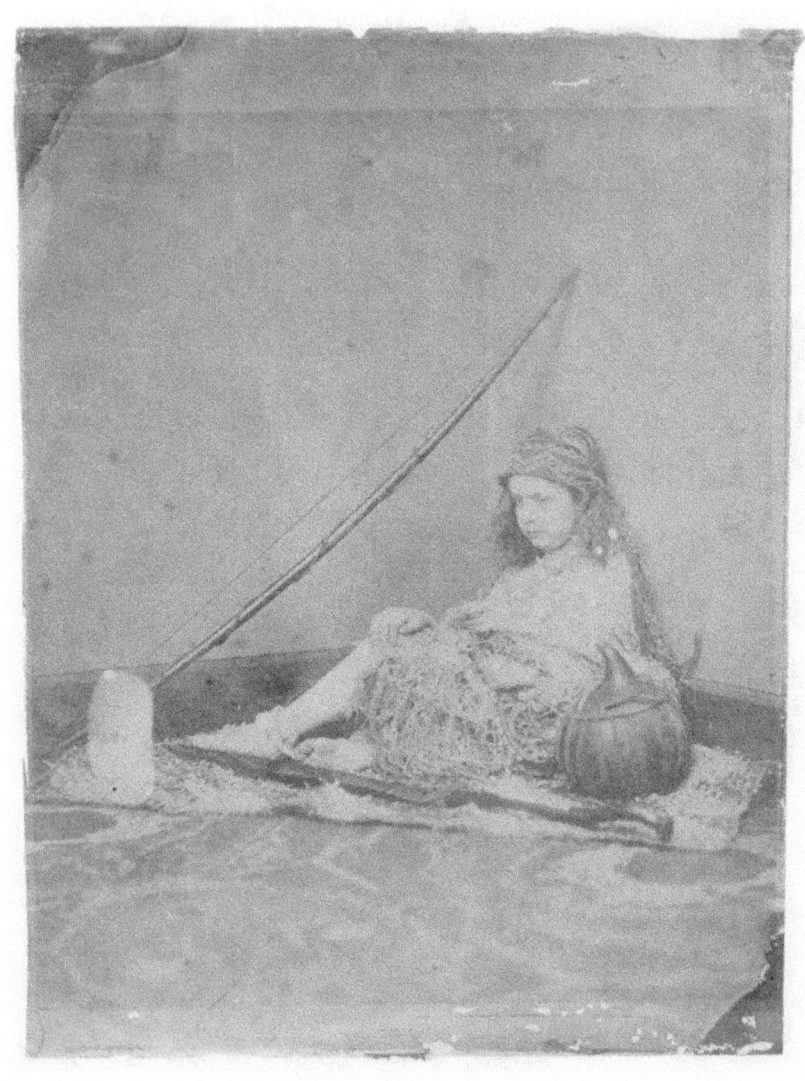

Ella Monier-Williams

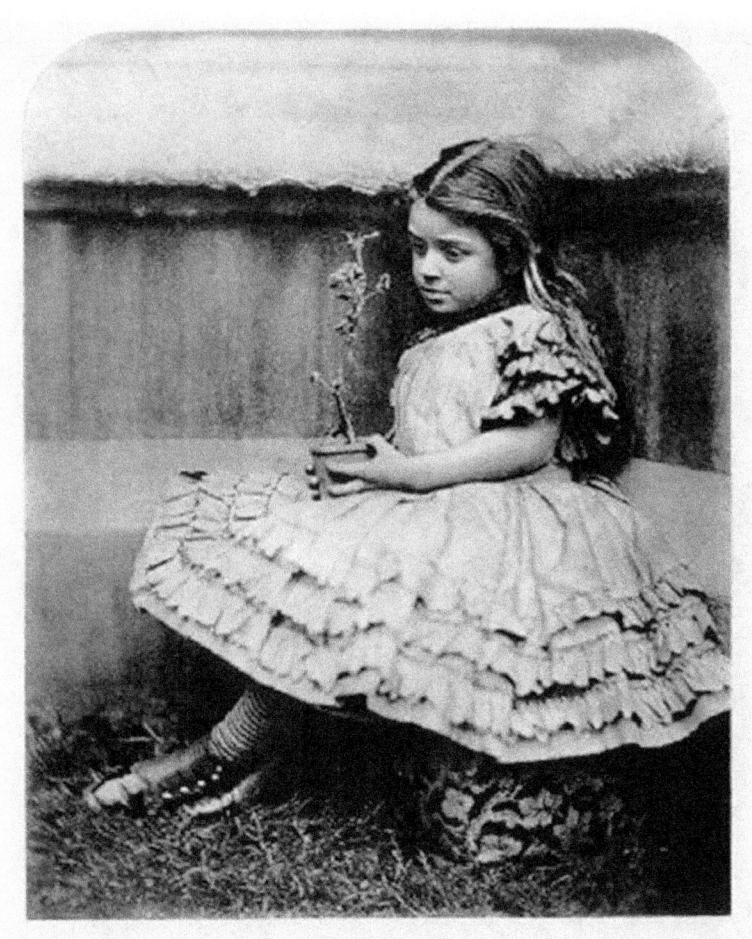

Maria White

Niece of the porter at Lambeth Palace.

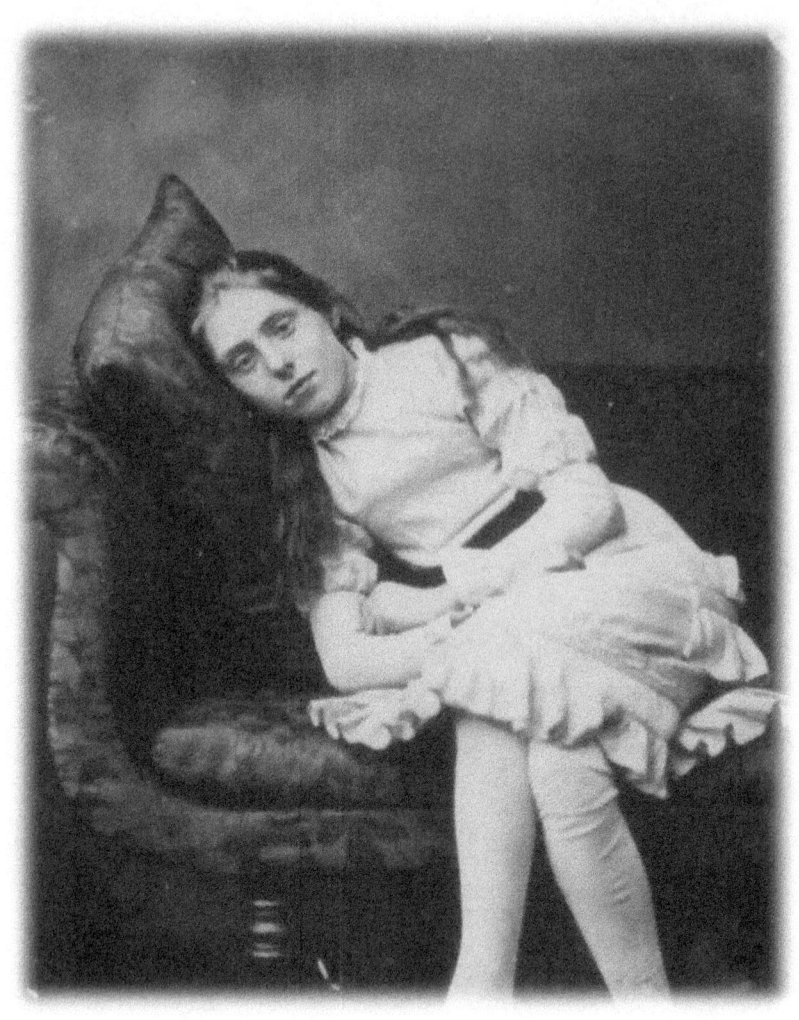
Leila Campbell

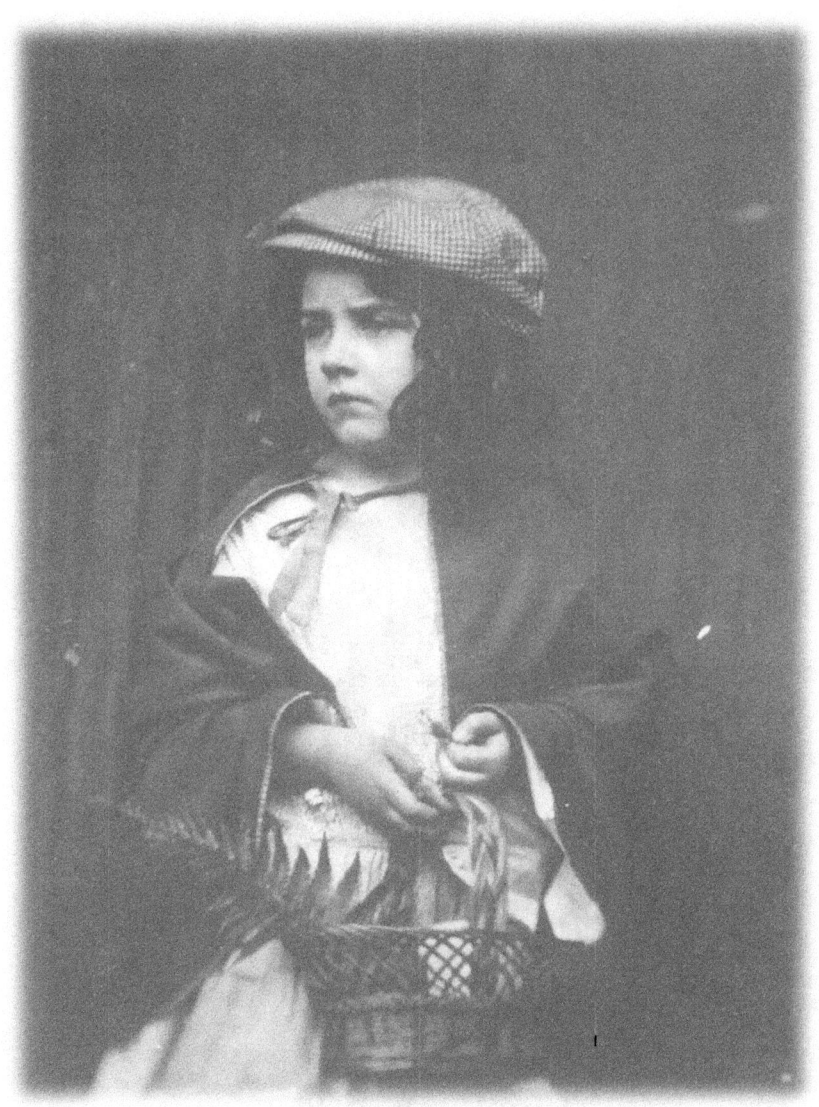

Young girl holding a basket

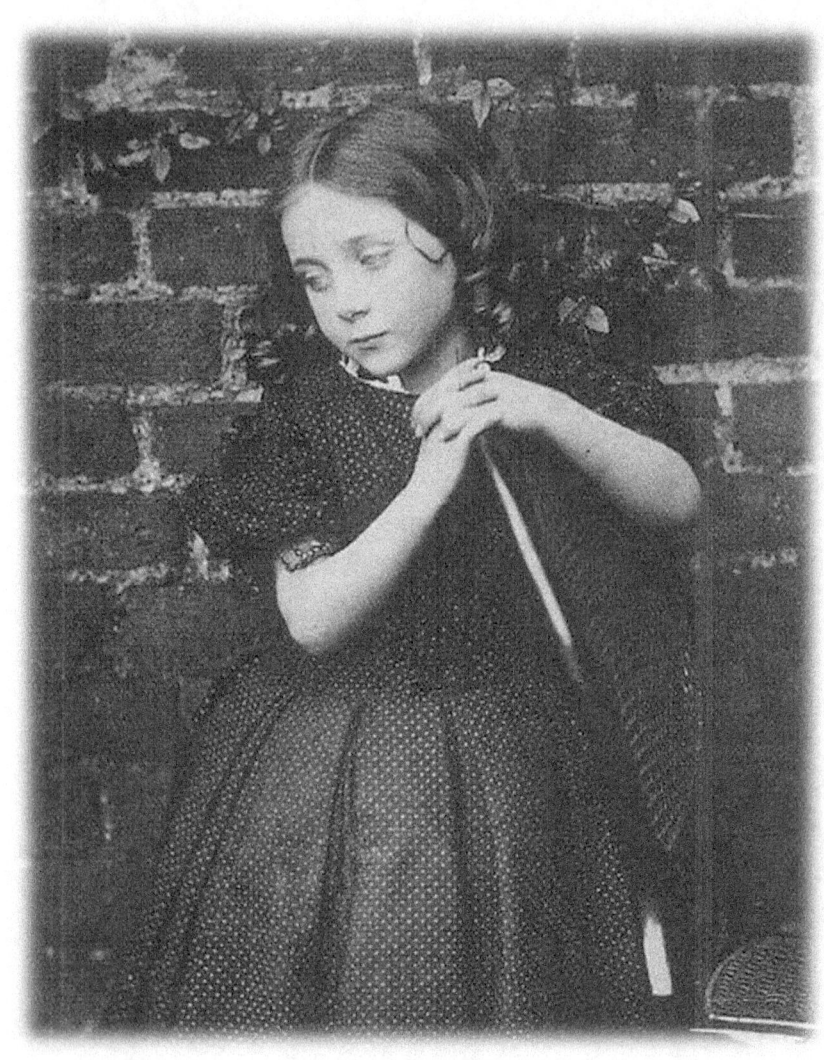

Amy Hughes 1863

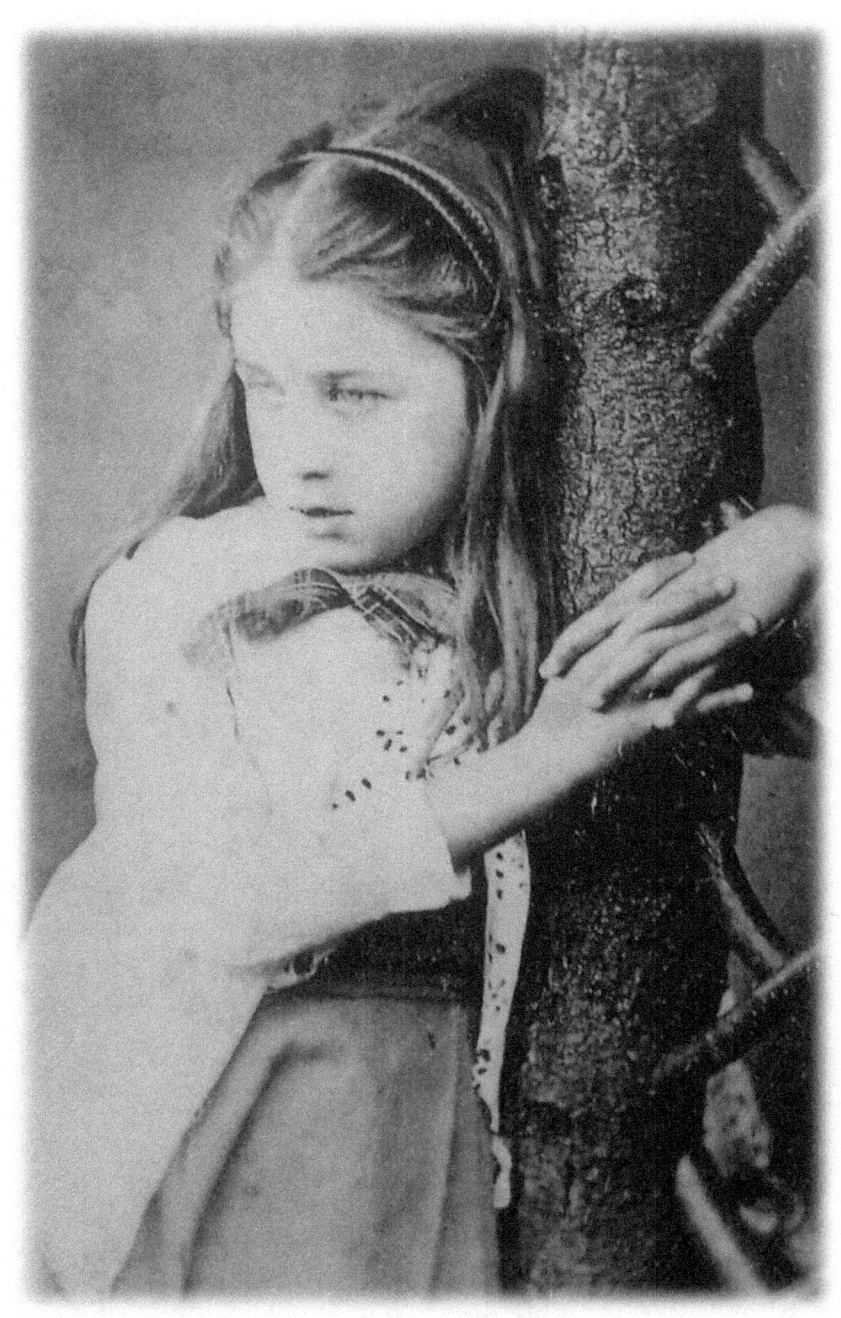

Edith Hulme 1869

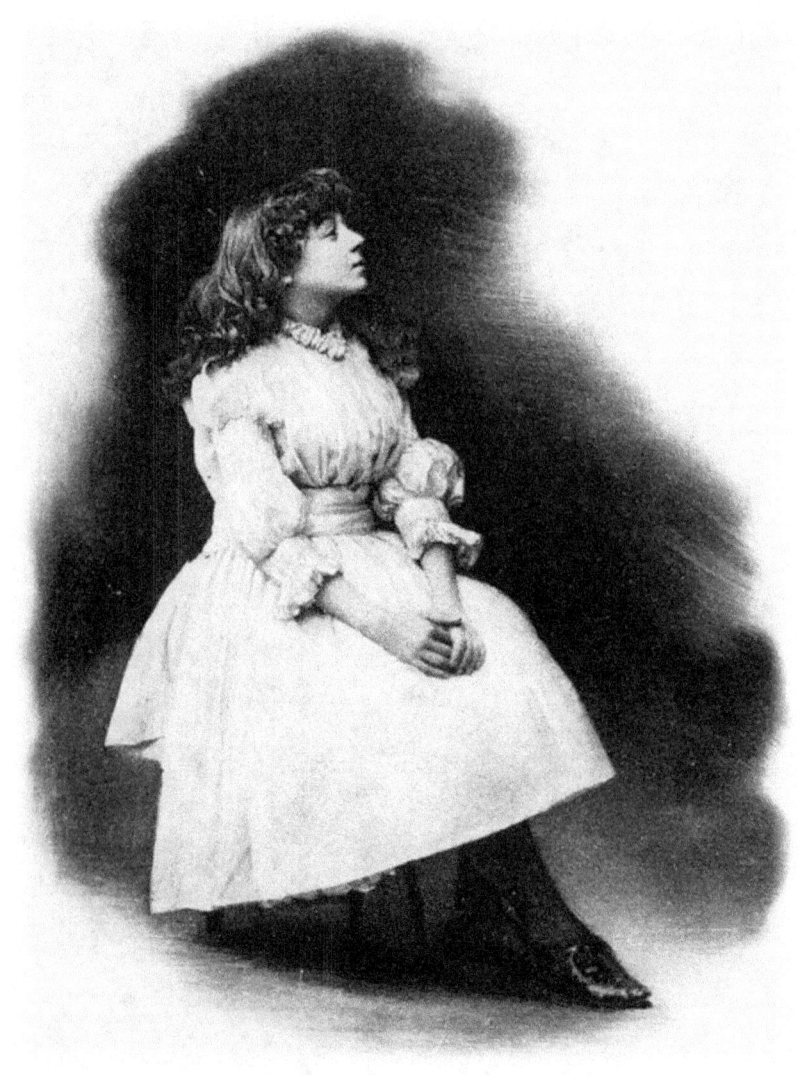

Isa Bowman (1874-1958)

Isa Bowman was an actress, a close friend of Lewis Carroll and author of a memoir about his life, The Story of Lewis Carroll, Told for Young People by the Real Alice in Wonderland. She met Carroll in 1886 when she played a small part in the stage version of Alice in Wonderland.

MEMOIR OF ISA BOWMAN

Memoir of Isa Bowman

Lewis Carroll was a man of medium height. When I knew him his hair was a silver-grey, rather longer than it was the fashion to wear, and his eyes were a deep blue. He was clean shaven, and, as he walked, always seemed a little unsteady in his gait. At Oxford he was a well-known figure. He was a little eccentric in his clothes. In the coldest weather he would never wear an overcoat, and he had a curious habit of always wearing, in all seasons of the year, a pair of grey and black cotton gloves.

But for the whiteness of his hair it was difficult to tell his age from his face, for there were no wrinkles on it. He had a curiously womanish face, and, in direct contradiction to his real character, there seemed to be little strength in it. One reads a great deal about the lines that a man's life paints in his face, and there are many people who believe that character is indicated by the curves of flesh and bone. I do not, and never shall, believe it is true, and Lewis Carroll is only one of many instances to support my theory. He was as firm and self-contained as a man may be, but there was little to show it in his face.

Yet you could easily discern it in the way in which he met and talked with his friends. When he shook hands with you--he had firm white hands, rather large--his grip was strong and steadfast. Every one knows the kind of man of whom it is said "his hands were all soft and flabby when he said, 'How-do-you-do.'" Well, Lewis Carroll was not a bit like that. Every one says when he shook your hand the pressure of his was full of strength, and you felt here indeed was a man to admire and to love. The expression in his eyes was also very kind and charming.

He used to look at me, when we met, in the very tenderest, gentlest way. Of course on an ordinary occasion I knew that his interested glance did not mean anything of any extra importance. Nothing could have happened since I had seen him last, yet, at the same time, his look was always so deeply sympathetic and benevolent that one could hardly help feeling it meant a great deal more than the expression of the ordinary man.

He was afflicted with what I believe is known as "Housemaid's knee," and this made his movements singularly jerky and abrupt. Then again he found it impossible to avoid stammering in his speech. He would, when engaged in an animated conversation with a friend, talk quickly and well for a few minutes, and then suddenly and without any very apparent cause would begin to stutter so much, that it was often difficult to understand him. He was very conscious of this impediment, and he tried hard to cure himself. For several years he read a scene from some play of Shakespeare's every day aloud, but despite this he was never quite able to cure himself of the habit. Many people would have found this a great hindrance to the affairs of ordinary life, and would have felt it deeply. Lewis Carroll was different. His mind and life were so simple and open that there was no room in them for self-consciousness, and I have often heard him jest at his own misfortune, with a comic wonder at it.

The personal characteristic that you would notice most on meeting Lewis Carroll was his extreme shyness. With children, of course, he was not nearly so reserved, but in the society of people of maturer age he was almost old-maidishly prim in his manner. When he knew a child well this reserve would vanish completely, but it needed only a slightly disconcerting incident to bring the cloak of shyness about him once more, and close the lips that just before had been talking so delightfully.

I shall never forget one afternoon when we had been walking in Christ Church meadows. On one side of the great open space the little river Cherwell runs through groves of trees towards the Isis, where the college boat-races are rowed. We were going quietly along by the side of the "Cher," when he began to explain to me that the tiny stream was a tributary, "a baby river" he put it, of the big Thames. He talked for some minutes, explaining how rivers came down from hills and flowed eventually to the sea, when he suddenly met a brother Don at a turning in the avenue.

He was holding my hand and giving me my lesson in geography with great earnestness when the other man came round the corner.

He greeted him in answer to his salutation, but the incident disturbed his train of thought, and for the rest of the walk he became very difficult to understand, and talked in a nervous and preoccupied manner. One strange way in which his nervousness affected him was peculiarly characteristic. When, owing to the stupendous success of "Alice in Wonderland" and "Alice Through the Looking-Glass," he became a celebrity many people were anxious to see him, and in some way or other to find out what manner of man he was. This seemed to him horrible, and he invented a mild deception for use when some autograph-hunter or curious person sent him a request for his signature on a photograph, or asked him some silly question as to the writing of one of his books, how long it took to write, and how many copies had been sold. Through some third person he always represented that Lewis Carroll the author and Mr. Dodgson the professor were two distinct persons, and that the author could not be heard of at Oxford at all. On one occasion an American actually wrote to say that he had heard that Lewis Carroll had laid out a garden to represent some of the scenes in "Alice in Wonderland," and that he (the American) was coming right away to take photographs of it. Poor Lewis Carroll, he was in terror of Americans for a week!

Of being photographed he had a horror, and despite the fact that he was continually and importunately requested to sit before the camera, only very few photographs of him are in existence. Yet he had been himself a great amateur photographer, and had taken many pictures that were remarkable in their exact portraiture of the subject.

It was this exactness that he used to pride himself on in his camera work. He always said that modern professional photographers spoilt all their pictures by touching them up absurdly to flatter the sitter. When it was necessary for me to have some pictures taken he sent me to Mr. H. H. Cameron, whom he declared to be the only artist who dared to produce a photograph that was exactly like its subject.

Miss Beatrice Hatch, to whose kindness I am indebtedfor much interesting information, writes in the Strand Magazine (April 1898):

"My earliest recollections of Mr. Dodgson are connected with photography. He was very fond of this art at one time, though he had entirely given it up for many years latterly. He kept various costumes and 'properties' with which to dress us up, and, of course, that added to the fun. What child would not thoroughly enjoy personating a Japanese or a beggar child, or a gipsy or an Indian? Sometimes there were excursions to the roof of the college, which was easily accessible from the windows of the studio. Or you might stand by your friend's side in the tiny dark room and watch him while he poured the contents of several little strong-smelling bottles on to the glass picture of yourself that looked so funny with its black face."

Yet, despite his love for the photographer's art, he hated the idea of having his own picture taken for the benefit of a curious world. The shyness that made him nervous in the presence of strangers made the idea that any one who cared to stare into a shop window could examine and criticise his portrait extremely repulsive to him.

I remember that this shyness of his was the only occasion of anything approaching a quarrel between us.

I had an idle trick of drawing caricatures when I was a child, and one day when he was writing some letters I began to make a picture of him on the back of an envelope. I quite forget what the drawing was like--probably it was an abominable libel--but suddenly he turned round and saw what I was doing. He got up from his seat and turned very red, frightening me very much. Then he took my poor little drawing, and tearing it into small pieces threw it into the fire without a word. Afterwards he came suddenly to me, and saying nothing, caught me up in his arms and kissed me passionately. I was only some ten or eleven years of age at the time, but now the incident comes back to me very clearly, and I can see it as if it happened but yesterday--the sudden snatching of my picture, the hurried striding across the room, and then the tender light in his face as he caught me up to him and kissed me.

I used to see a good deal of him at Oxford, and I was constantly in Christ Church. He would invite me to stay with him and find me rooms just outside the college gates, where I was put into charge of an elderly dame, whose name, if I do not forget, was Mrs. Buxall. I would spend long happy days with my uncle, and at nine o'clock I was taken over to the little house in St. Aldates and delivered into the hands of the landlady, who put me to bed.

In the morning I was awakened by the deep reverberations of "Great Tom" calling Oxford to wake and begin the new day. Those times were very pleasant, and the remembrance of them lingers with me still. Lewis Carroll at the time of which I am speaking had two tiny turret rooms, one on each side of his staircase in Christ Church. He always used to tell me that when I grew up and became married he would give me the two little rooms, so that if I ever disagreed with my husband we could each of us retire to a turret till we had made up our quarrel!

And those rooms of his! I do not think there was ever such a fairy-land for children. I am sure they must have contained one of the finest collections of musical-boxes to be found anywhere in the world. There were big black ebony boxes with glass tops through which you could see all the works. There was a big box with a handle, which it was quite hard exercise for a little girl to turn, and there must have been twenty or thirty little ones which could only play one tune. Sometimes one of the musical-boxes would not play properly, and then I always got tremendously excited. Uncle used to go to a drawer in the table and produce a box of little screw-drivers and punches, and while I sat on his knee he would unscrew the lid and take out the wheels to see what was the matter. He must have been a clever mechanist, for the result was always the same-after a longer or shorter period the music began again. Sometimes when the musical-boxes had played all their tunes he used to put them in the box backwards, and was as pleased as I at the comic effect of the music "standing on its head," as he phrased it.

There was another and very wonderful toy which he sometimes produced for me, and this was known as "The Bat." The ceilings of the rooms in which he lived at the time were very high indeed, and admirably suited for the purposes of "The Bat." It was an ingeniously constructed toy of gauze and wire, which actually flew about the room like a bat. It was worked by a piece of twisted elastic, and it could fly for about half a minute.

I was always a little afraid of this toy because it was too lifelike, but there was a fearful joy in it. When the music-boxes began to pall he would get up from his chair and look at me with a knowing smile. I always knew what was coming even before he began to speak, and I used to dance up and down in tremendous anticipation.

"Isa, my darling," he would say, "once upon a time there was some one called Bob the Bat! and he lived in the top left-hand drawer of the writing-table. What could he do when uncle wound him up?" And then I would squeak out breathlessly, "He could really FLY!" Bob the Bat had many adventures. There was no way of controlling the direction of its flight, and one morning, a hot summer's morning when the window was wide open, Bob flew out into the garden and alighted in a bowl of salad which a scout was taking to some one's rooms. The poor fellow was so startled by the sudden flapping apparition that he dropped the bowl, and it was broken into a thousand pieces.

There! I have written "a thousand pieces," and a thoughtless exaggeration of that sort was a thing that Lewis Carroll hated. "A thousand pieces?" he would have said; "you know, Isa, that if the bowl had been broken into a thousand pieces they would each have been so tiny that you could have hardly seen them." And if the broken pieces had been get-at-able, he would have made me count them as a means of impressing on my mind the folly of needless exaggeration.

I remember how annoyed he was once when, after a morning's sea bathing at Eastbourne, I exclaimed, "Oh, this salt water, it always makes my hair as stiff as a poker."

He impressed it on me quite irritably that no little girl's hair could ever possibly get as stiff as a poker. "If you had said, 'as stiff as wires,' it would have been more like it, but even that would have been an exaggeration." And then, seeing that I was a little frightened, he drew for me a picture of "The little girl called Isa whose hair turned into pokers because she was always exaggerating things."

That, and all the other pictures that he drew for me are, I'm sorry to say, the sole property of the little fishes in the Irish Channel, where a clumsy porter dropped them as we hurried into the boat at Holyhead.

"I nearly died of laughing," was another expression that he particularly disliked; in fact any form of exaggeration generally called from him a reproof, though he was sometimes content to make fun. For instance, my sisters and I had sent him "millions of kisses" in a letter. Below you will find the letter that he wrote in return, written in violet ink that he always used (dreadfully ugly, I used to think it).

"CH. Ch. Oxford, "_Ap. 14, 1890_.

"MY OWN DARLING,

It's all very well for you and Nellie and Emsie to write in millions of hugs and kisses, but please consider the time it would occupy your poor old very busy Uncle!

Try hugging and kissing Emsie for a minute by the watch, and I don't think you'll manage it more than 20 times a minute.

'Millions' must mean 2 millions at least.

20)2,000,000 hugs and kisses
60)100,000 minutes
12)1,666 hours
6)138 days (at twelve hours a day)
23 weeks.

I couldn't go on hugging and kissing more than 12 hours a day: and I wouldn't like to spend Sundays that way. So you see it would take 23 weeks of hard work. Really, my dear child, I cannot spare the time .

Why haven't I written since my last letter? Why, how _could_ I, you silly silly child? How could I have written since the last time I did write? Now, you just try it with kissing. Go and kiss Nellie, from me, several times, and take care to manage it so as to have kissed her since the last time you _did_ kiss her. Now go back to your place, and I'll question you.

'Have you kissed her several times?'

'Yes, darling Uncle.'

'What o'clock was it when you gave her the last kiss?'

'5 minutes past 10, Uncle.'

'Very well, now, have you kissed her since?'

'Well--I--ahem! ahem! ahem! (excuse me, Uncle, I've got a bad cough). I--think--that--I--that is, you, know, I----'

'Yes, I see! "Isa" begins with "I," and it seems to me as if she was going to end with "I," this time!'

Anyhow, my not writing hasn't been because I was _ill_, but because I was a horrid lazy old thing, who kept putting it off from day to day, till at last I said to myself, 'WHO ROAR! There's no time to write now, because they sail on the 1st of April.' In fact, I shouldn't have been a bit surprised if this letter had been from Fulham, instead of Louisville. Well, I suppose you will be there by about the middle of May. But mind you don't write to me from there! Please, please, no more horrid letters from you! I do hate them so! And as for kissing them when I get them, why, I'd just as soon kiss--kiss--kiss you, you tiresome thing! So there now!

Thank you very much for those 2 photographs--I liked them--hum--pretty well. I can't honestly say I thought them the very best I had ever seen.

Please give my kindest regards to your mother, and 1/2 of a kiss to Nellie, and 1/200 a kiss to Emsie, and 1/2,000,000 a kiss to yourself. So, with fondest love, I am, my darling, your loving Uncle,

C. L. DODGSON."

And now, in the postscript, comes one of the rare instances in which Lewis Carroll showed his deep religious feeling. It runs--

P.S._--I've thought about that little prayer you asked me to write for Nellie and Emsie. But I would like, first, to have the words of the one I wrote for you , and the words of what they now say, if they say any. And then I will pray to our Heavenly Father to help me to write a prayer that will be really fit for them to use."

These letters are written in Lewis Carroll's ordinary handwriting, not a particularly legible one. When, however, he was writing for the press no characters could have been more clearly and distinctly formed than his. Throughout his life he always made it his care to give as little trouble as possible to other people.

"Why should the printers have to work overtime because my letters are ill-formed and my words run into each other?" he once said, when a friend remonstrated with him because he took such pains with the writing of his "copy." As a specimen of his careful penmanship the diary that he wrote for me, which is reproduced in this book in facsimile, is an admirable example.

They were happy days, those days in Oxford, spent with the most fascinating companion that a child could have. In our walks about the old town, in our visits to cathedral or chapel or hall, in our visits to his friends he was an ideal companion, but I think I was almost happiest when we came back to his rooms and had tea alone; when the fire-glow (it was always winter when I stayed in Oxford) threw fantastic shadows about the quaint room, and the thoughts of the prosiest of people must have wandered a little into fancy-land. The shifting firelight seemed to almost ætherealise that kindly face, and as the wonderful stories fell from his lips, and his eyes lighted on me with the sweetest smile that ever a man wore, I was conscious of a love and reverence for Charles Dodgson that became nearly an adoration.

It was almost pain when the lights were turned up and we came back to everyday life and tea.

He was very particular about his tea, which he always made himself, and in order that it should draw properly he would walk about the room swinging the tea-pot from side to side for exactly ten minutes. The idea of the grave professor promenading his book-lined study and carefully waving a tea-pot to and fro may seem ridiculous, but all the minutiæ of life received an extreme attention at his hands, and after the first surprise one came quickly to realise the convenience that his carefulness ensured.

Before starting on a railway journey, for instance (and how delightful were railway journeys in the company of Lewis Carroll), he used to map out exactly every minute of the time that we were to take on the way. The details of the journey completed, he would exactly calculate the amount of money that must be spent, and, in different partitions of the two purses that he carried, arrange the various sums that would be necessary for cabs, porters, newspapers, refreshments, and the other expenses of a journey. It was wonderful how much trouble he saved himself en route by thus making ready beforehand. Lewis Carroll was never driven half frantic on a station platform because he had to change a sovereign to buy a penny paper while the train was on the verge of starting. With him journeys were always comfortable.

For his little girl friends, of course, he reserved the most intimate side of his nature, but on occasion he would throw off his reserve and talk earnestly and well to some young man in whose life he took an interest.

Mr. Arthur Girdlestone is able to bear witness to this, and he has given me an account of an evening that he once spent with Lewis Carroll, which I reproduce here from notes made during our conversation.

Mr. Girdlestone, then an undergraduate at New College, had on one occasion to call on Lewis Carroll at his rooms in Tom Quad. At the time of which I am speaking Lewis Carroll had retired very much from the society which he had affected a few years before. Indeed for the last years of his life he was almost a recluse, and beyond dining in Hall saw hardly any one. Miss Beatrice Hatch, one of his "girl friends," writes apropos of his hermit-like seclusion:

"If you were very anxious to get him to come to your house on any particular day, the only chance was not to invite him, but only to inform him that you would be at home. Otherwise he would say, 'As you have invited me I cannot come, for I have made a rule to decline all invitations; but I will come the next day.' In former years he would sometimes consent to go to a 'party' if he was quite sure he was not to be 'shown off' or introduced to any one as the author of 'Alice.' I must again quote from a note of his in answer to an invitation to tea: 'What an awful proposition! To drink tea from four to six would tax the constitution even of a hardened tea drinker! For me, who hardly ever touch it, it would probably be fatal.'

"All through the University, except in an extremely limited circle, Lewis Carroll was regarded as a person who lived very much by himself.

"When I went to see him on quite a slight acquaintance, I confess it was with some slight feeling of trepidation. However I had to on some business, and accordingly I knocked at his door about 8.30 one winter's evening, and was invited to come in. "He was sitting working at a writing-table, and all round him were piles of MSS. arranged with mathematical neatness, and many of them tied up with tape. The lamp threw his face into sharp relief as he greeted me. My business was soon over, and I was about to go away, when he asked me if I would have a glass of wine and sit with him for a little.

"The night outside was very cold, and the fire was bright and inviting, and I sat down. He began to talk to me of ordinary subjects, of the things a man might do at Oxford, of the place itself, and the affection in which he held it. He talked quietly, and in a rather tired voice. During our conversation my eye fell upon a photograph of a little girl--evidently from the freshness of its appearance but newly taken--which was resting upon the ledge of a reading-stand at my elbow. It was the picture of a tiny child, very pretty, and I picked it up to look at it.

"'That is the baby of a girl friend of mine,' he said, and then, with an absolute change of voice, 'there is something very strange about very young children, something I cannot understand.' I asked him in what way, and he explained at some length. He was far less at his ease than when talking trivialities, and he occasionally stammered and sometimes hesitated for a word. I cannot remember all he said, but some of his remarks still remain with me. He said that in the company of very little children his brain enjoyed a rest which was startlingly recuperative. If he had been working too hard or had tired his brain in any way, to play with children was like an actual material tonic to his whole system. I understood him to say that the effect was almost physical!

"He said that he found it much easier to understand children, to get his mind into correspondence with their minds when he was fatigued with other work. Personally, I did not understand little children, and they seemed quite outside my experience, and rather incautiously I asked him if children never bored him. He had been standing up for most of the time, and when I asked him that, he sat down suddenly. 'They are three-fourths of my life,' he said. 'I cannot understand how any one could be bored by little children. I think when you are older you will come to see this--I hope you'll come to see it.'

"After that he changed the subject once more, and became again the mathematician--a little formal, and rather weary."

The Story of Lewis Carroll Told For Young People By The Real Alice In Wonderland, Carroll's young friend Isa Bowman

THE MAN BEHIND THE CAMERA

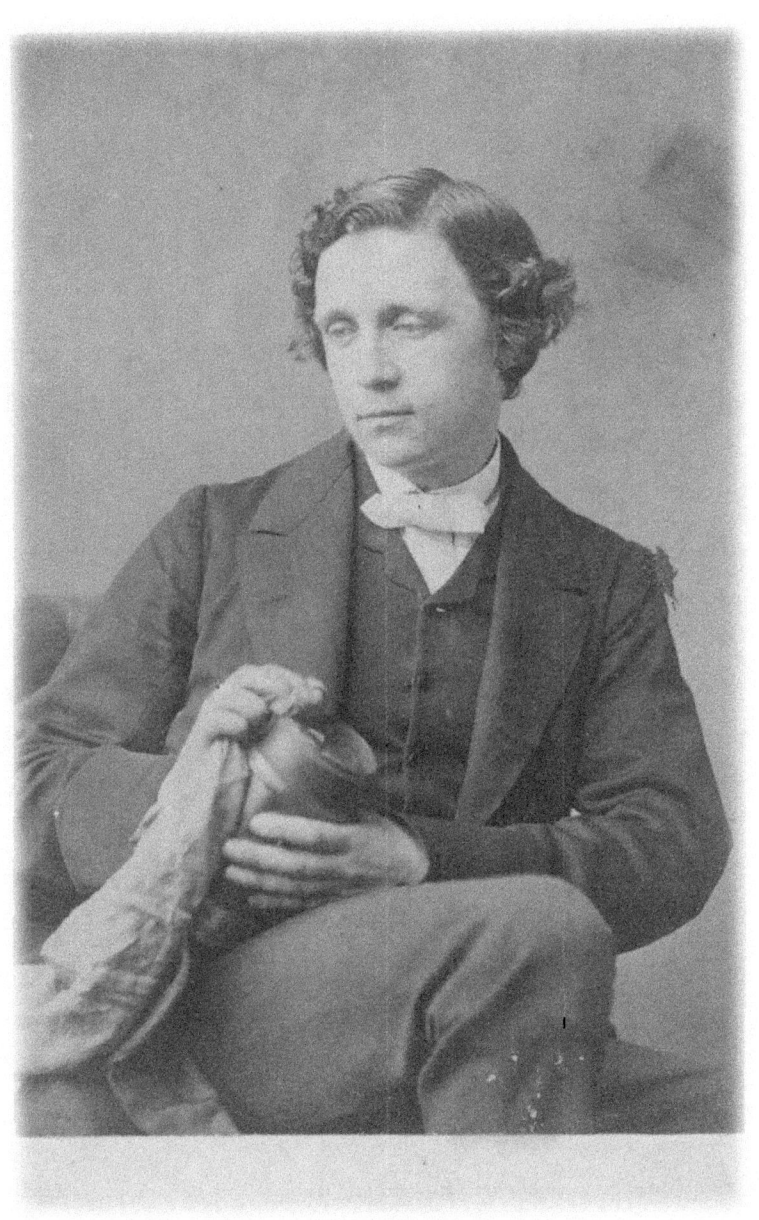

Lewis Carroll

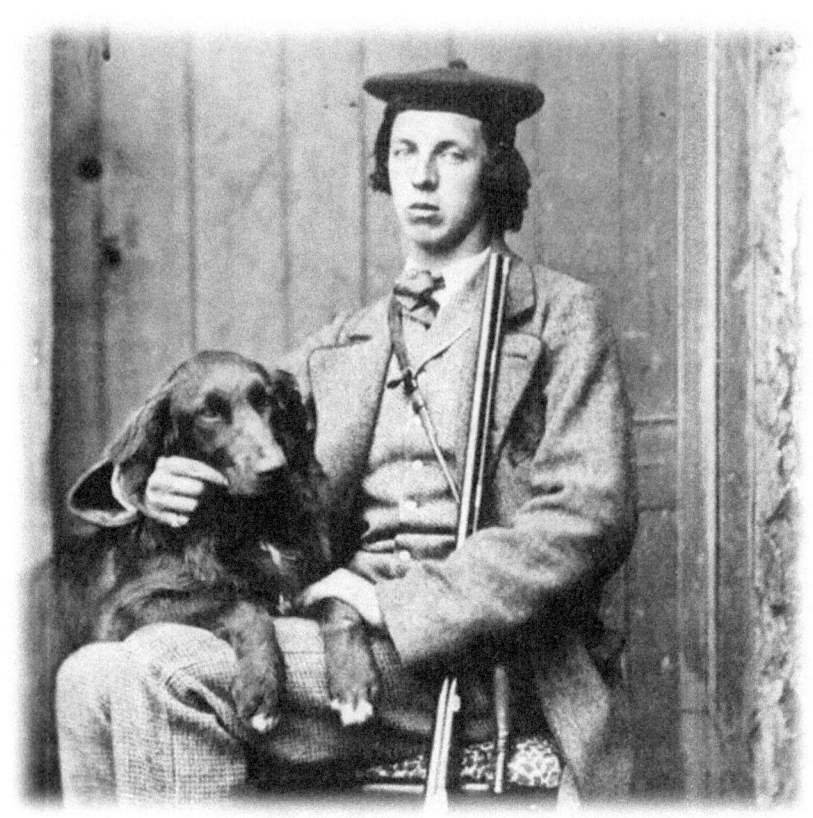

Lewis Carroll

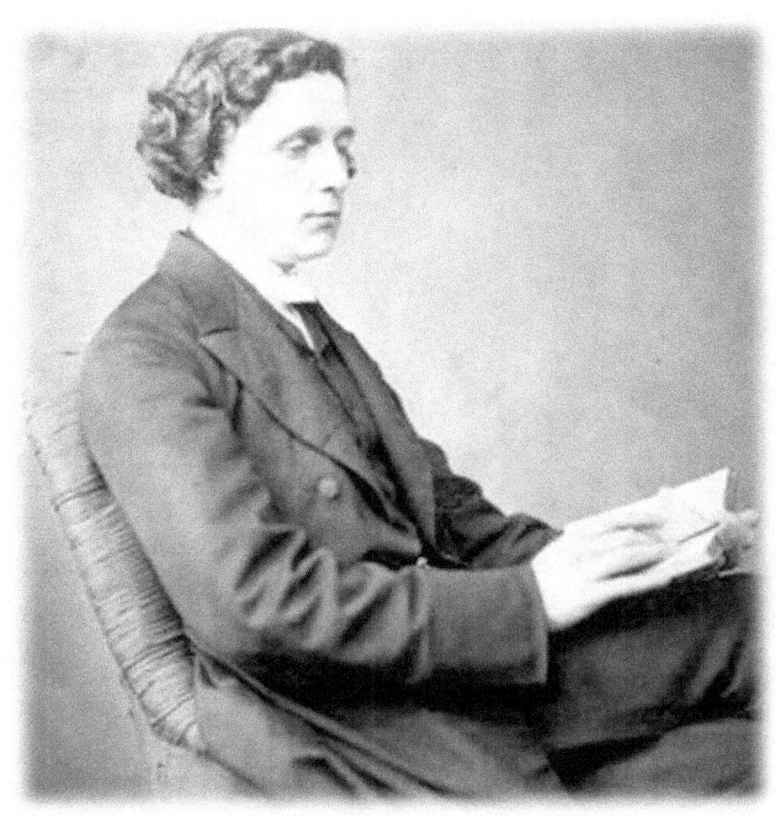

Lewis Carroll

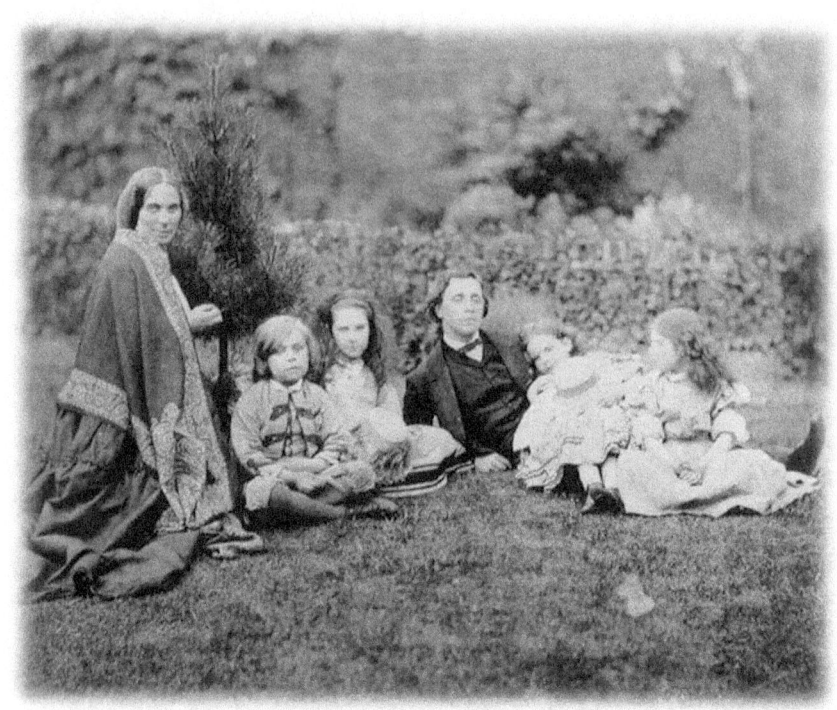

Lewis Carroll the Governess and little friends

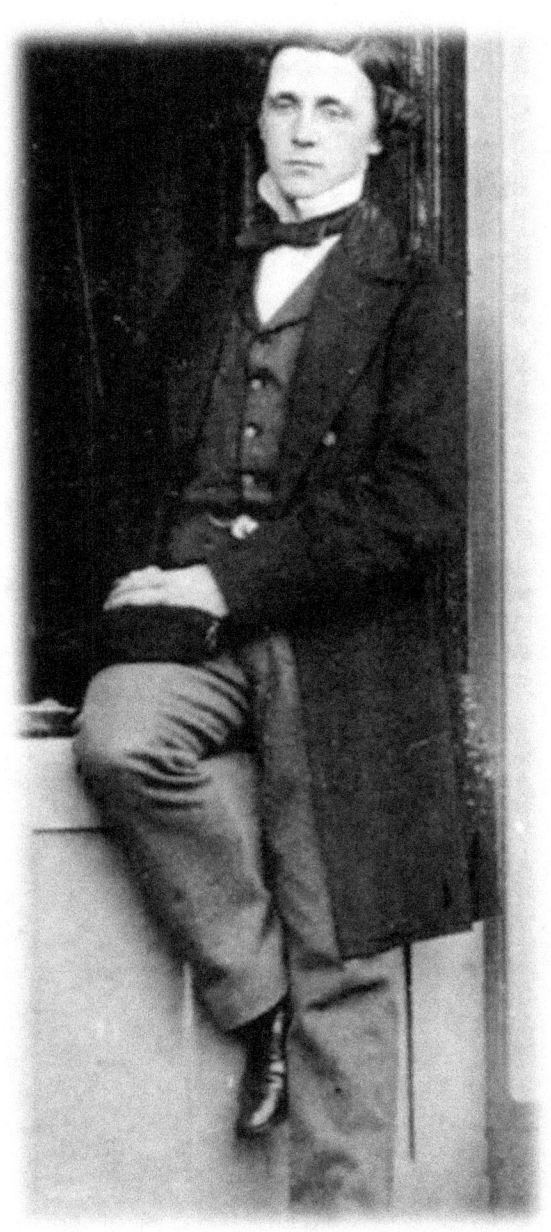
Lewis Carroll

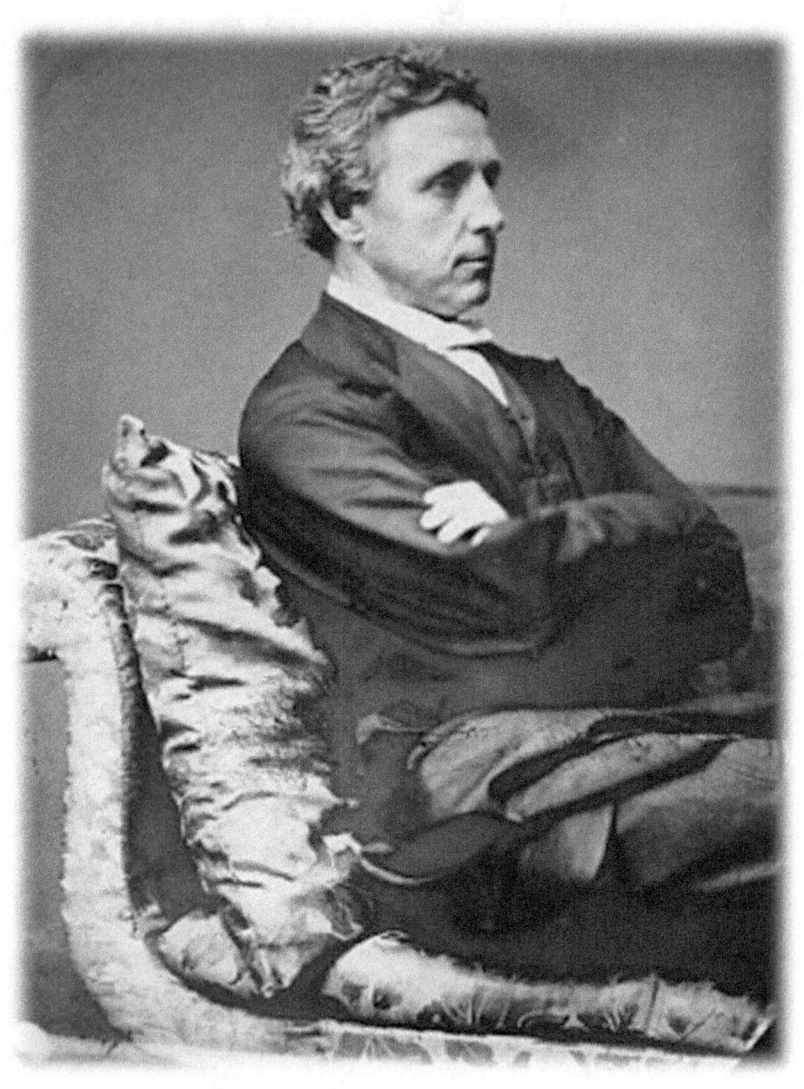

Lewis Carroll (1832-1898)

QUOTATIONS FROM A SELECTION FROM THE LETTERS OF LEWIS CARROLL

Quotations from *A Selection from the Letters of Lewis Carroll to his Child-Friends* (1933) edited by Evelyn M. Hatch

- It's been so frightfully hot here that been almost too weak to hold a pen, and even if I had been able, there was no ink — it had all evaporated into a cloud of black steam, and in that state it has been floating about the room, inking the walls and ceiling; till they're hardly fit to be seen: to-day it is cooler, and a little has come back into the ink-bottle in the form of black snow.
  - Letter to Mary MacDonald (23 May 1864), p.22

- The only unlucky thing that happened to me was *your* writing to me. There!
  - Letter to Mary MacDonald (23 May 1864), p.23

- They did things very simply in those days: if you had a lot of money, you just dug a hole under the hedge, and popped it in: then you said you had "put it in the bank"
  - Letter to Mary MacDonald (14 November 1864), p.24

- Do not suppose I didn't *write*, hundreds of times; the difficulty has been with the *directing* - I directed the letters so violently at first, that they went far beyond the mark - some of them were picked up at the other end of Russia.
  - Letter to Mary MacDonald (5 December 1864), pp.24-5

- My room is very easy to find when you get here, and as for *distance*, you know - why, Oxford is as near to

London as London is to Oxford. If your geography-book doesn't tell you *that*, it must be a wretched affair.
  - Letter to Mary MacDonald (22 January 1866), p.26

- The book has got a moral - so I need hardly say it is *not* by Lewis Carroll.
  - Letter to Lily MacDonald (5 January 1867), p.34

- As to your all having grown so old that I no longer care for you, a difficulty occurs to me: *can* you leave off caring for people before you have begun?
  - Letter to Lily MacDonald (3 April 1870), p.35

- What is "F" before "Dymphna"? Is it Fatima, Fenella or Feodora? or is it (I hardly dare hope for so beautiful a name) Foscofornia?
  - Letter to Dymphna Ellis (3 Aug 1865), p.40

- I found out that she was called "Maggie" and lived in a Crescent! Of course I declared "After *that*" (the language I used doesn't matter), "I will *not* address her, that's flat! So do not expect me to flatter!"
  - Letter to Maggie Cunnynghame (30 January 1868), p.42

- No *carte* has yet been done of me that does real justice to my *smile*; and so I hardly like, you see, to send you one - however, I'll Consider if I will or not - meanwhile I send a little thing to give you an idea of what I look like when I'm lecturing. The merest sketch, you will allow - yet I still think there's something grand in the expression of the brow and in the action of the hand.
  - Letter to Maggie Cunnynghame (30 January 1868), p.42

- My best love to yourself - to your mother my kindest regards - to your small, fat, impertinent, ignorant brother my hatred.
  - Letter to Maggie Cunnynghame (30 January 1868), p.43

- I hope to come and see you for about half an hour on the 3rd of July 1872.
  - Letter to Dolly Argles (222 April 1868), p.50; thus he was hoping to visit her in over four years.

- Some children have a most disagreeable way of getting grown-up: I hope you won't do anything of that sort before we meet again.
  - Letter to Dolly Argles (28? April 1868), p.52

- "Don't talk to me of going quick," said Fox, "you howling Hound!
  My feet are done with patent glue, that sticks them to the ground."
  - Letter to Dolly Argles (29 April 1868), p.54

- You say you "hope you will soon see me." That depends on yourself: if when I come, you look carefully the other way and never turn your head round, it wil probably be a long time before you see me.
  - Letter to Dolly Argles (3 January 1869), p.58

- A friend of mine, called Mr. Lewis Carroll, tells me he means to send you a book. He is a *very* dear friend of mine. I have known him all my life (we are the same age) and have *never* left him. Of course he was with me in the Gardens, not a yard off—even while I was drawing those puzzles for you. I wonder if you saw him?
  - Letter to Isabel Standen (22 August 1869), p.69

- I did make an explanation once for "uffish thought" - It seems to suggest a state of mind when the voice is

gruffish, the manner roughish, and the temper huffish.
  - Letter to Maud Standen (18 December 1877), p.73

- Some of my friends are business-men, and it is pleasant to see how methodical and careful they are in transacting any business matter. If, for instance, one of them were to write to me, asking me to look out for a place for a French governess in whom he was interested, I should be sure to admire the care with which he would give me *her name in full* (in extra-legible writing if it were an unusual name) as well as her address.

  Some of my friends are not men of business.

  - Letter to Isabel Standen (5 July 1885), p.75

- He thought you might be "*thirty*" not "*thirteen.*" "No child of thirteen ever wrote such a hand as that" he cried. However I told him you certainly were a child, and that you had been to a very good school at the bottom of the sea.
  - Letter to Mary Marshall (19 April 1870), p.79

- The great question is, do you generally think right or wrong? *I* should say (judging by the experience of many years) *wrong, almost always.*
  - Letter to Janet Merriman (17 December 1870), p.80

- "Why can't you make up *your* mind?" that's a riddle I've just invented. "Because you haven't got one to make up" - that's the answer to it, only you'd never have guessed it.
  - Letter to Janet Merriman (17 December 1870), p.80

- It is a great shock to my sensitive feelings to find that young ladies (of a certain age, and engaged) persist in signing themselves "very affectionately": it shows a

grievous disregard of the very rudiments of conventionalism; but how can *I* help it? Against such mighty forces, what avail the feeble efforts of *Man*?
  - Letter to Ella Monier-Williams (29 April 1880), p.89

- My name is spelt with a "G," that is to say "*Dodgson*." Any one who spells it the same as that wretch (I mean of course the Chairman of Committees in the House of Commons) offends me *deeply*, and *for ever!* It is a thing I *can* forget, but *never can forgive!*
  - Letter to Gaynor Simpson (27 December 1873), p.90

- As to dancing, my dear, I *never* dance, unless I am allowed to do it *in my own peculiar way*. There is no use trying to describe it: it has to be seen to be believed. The last house I tried it in, the floor broke through. But then it was a poor sort of floor — the beams were only six inches thick, hardly worth calling beams at all: stone arches are much more sensible, when any dancing, *of my peculiar kind*, is to be done. Did you ever see the Rhinoceros, and the Hippopotamus, at the Zoological Gardens, trying to dance a minuet together? It is a touching sight.

  Give any message from me to Amy that you think will be most likely to surprise her.

  - Letter to Gaynor Simpson (27 December 1873), pp.90-1

- What an awful proposition! To drink tea from 4 to 6 would tax the constitution even of a hardened tea-drinker. For me, who hardly ever touch it, it would probably be fatal.
  - Letter to Mrs. Bessie Hatch (14 May 1873), p.94

- What remarkably wicked children you are! I don't think you would find in all history, even if you go back to the times of Nero and Heliogabalus, any instance of children so heartless and so entirely

reckless about returning story-books. Now I think of it, neither Nero nor Heliogabalus ever failed to return any story-book they borrowed. That is certain, because they never borrowed any, and that again is certain because there were none printed in those days.
- Letter to Julia and Ethel Arnold (1874), p.96

- At last I met a wheelbarrow that I thought would attend to me, but I couldn't make out what was in it. I saw some features at first, then I looked through a telescope, and found it was a countenance; then I looked through a microscope, and found it was a face! I thought it was rather like me, so I fetched a large looking-glass to make sure, and then to my great joy I found it was me. We shook hands, and were just beginning to talk, when myself came up and joined us, and we had quite a pleasant conversation.
  - Letter to Magdalen Williams (15 December 1875), pp.97-8

- Of course you know what a Snark is? If you do, please tell *me:* for I haven't an idea what it is like.
  - Letter to Florence Balfour (6 April 1876), pp.98-9

- As are the feelings of the old lady who, after feeding her canary and going out for a walk, finds the cage entirely filled on her return, with a live turkey - or of the old gentleman who, after chaining up a small terrier overnight, finds a hippopotamus raging round the kennel in the morning - such are my feelings when, trying to recall the memory of a small child who went to wade in the sea at Sandown, I meet with the astonishing photograph of the same microcosm suddenly expanded into a tall young person, whom I should be too shy to look at, even with the telescope which would no doubt be necessary to get any distinct idea of her smile, or at any rate to satisfy oneself whether she had eyebrows or not!
  - Letter to Florence Balfour (10 Feb 1882), p.99

- I'm down here all alone, but as happy as a king - at least, as happy as *some* kings - at any rate I should think I'm about as happy as King Charles the First when he was in prison.
    - Letter to his cousin Menella Wilcox (20 July 1886), p.127

- Hateful Spider, (You are quite right. It doesn't matter a bit how one begins a letter, nor, for the matter of that, how one goes on with it, or even how one ends it - and it comes awfully easy, after a bit, to write coldly - easier, if possible, than to write warmly. For instance, I have been writing to the Dean, on College business, and began the letter "Obscure Animalcule," and he is foolish enough to pretend to be angry about it, and to say it wasn't a proper style, and that he will propose to the Vice-Chancellor to expel me from the University: and it is all your fault!)
    - Letter to Agnes Hull (30 April 1881), p.149

- I may as well just tell you a few of the things I like, and then, whenever you want to give me a birthday present (my birthday comes once every seven years, on the fifth Tuesday in April) you will know what to give me. Well, I like, very much indeed, a little mustard with a bit of beef spread thinly under it; and I like brown sugar - only it should have some apple pudding mixed with it to keep it from being too sweet; but perhaps what I like best of all is salt, with some soup poured over it. The use of the soup is to hinder the salt from being too dry; and it helps to melt it. Then there are other things I like; for instance, pins - only they should always have a cushion put round them to keep them warm. And I like two or three handfuls of hair; only they should always have a little girl's head beneath them to grow on, or else whenever you open the door they get blown all over the room, and then they get lost, you know.
    - Letter to Jessie Sinclair (22 Jan 1878), pp.154-5

- I shall be very glad to hear from you whenever you feel inclined to write, and from Sally, too, if *she* likes to try her had at writing. If she can't write with her hand, let her try with her foot.
  - Letter to Jessie Sinclair (22 Jan 1878), pp.155-6

- I get about 2000 letters off, every year; but it isn't enough!
  - Letter to Mary Brown (22 Jan 1878), p.169

- To say that I am quite well "goes without saying" with me. In fact my life is so strangely free from all trials & troubles, that I cannot doubt my own happiness is one of the "talents" entrusted to me to "occupy" wirh, till the Master shal return, by doing something to make "other" lives happy.
  - Letter to Mary Brown (22 Jan 1878), p.170

- Why she should die, Mr. Tennyson only knows! I suppose he would say, "It gives a roundness and finish to the thing." So it may; but a heroine who would poison herself for that must have an almost morbid fondness for roundness and finish.
  - On the heroine committing suicide in Tennyson's play "The Cup"
  - Letter to Helen Feilden (12 Apr 1881), p.173

- I have a good many friends among governesses - having a sort of sympathy with them, as a more or less down-trodden race.
  - Letter to Mrs. Richards (13 Mar 1882), p.177

- *Do* we decide questions, at all? We decide *answers*, no doubt; but surely the questions decide us?
  - Letter to Marion Richards (8 Feb 1886), p.178

- I must find a few minutes to offer you the very sincere wishes of an old friend that your married life may be a bright and peaceful one, andd that you and your chosen husband may love each other with a love second only to your love of God and far above your

love of any other object. For *that* is, I believe, the only *essential* for a happily married life: All else is trivial compared with it.
  - Letter to Kate Terry Lewis (4 July 1893), p.180

- And will you then resign yourself to Fate and me, to be taken either to a Matinée or to the General Strike Meeting of the London Omnibus Company, whichever I find to be most expedient?
  - Letter to Beatrice Earle (3 June 1891), p.183

- It is as much as I can do to find time to draw the corks of the bottles of beer I consume - and as for drawing *children*, it's out of the question!
  - Letter to Ethel Hatch (19 Aug 1884), p.189

- Oh woman, in our hours of ease
  A most unmitigated tease!
  When pain and anguish wring the brow,
  Doesn't she make a jolly row?
  - Letter to Kitty Savile Clark, parodying Sir <u>Walter Scott</u> (29 November 1888), p.191

- That anyone should look up to *me*, or think of asking *my* advice - well, it makes one feel humble, I think, rather than proud - humble to remember, while others think so well of me, what I really *am*, in myself.
  - Letter to Edith Rix (1887), p.195

- My dear Winnie,
  But you will be getting tired of this long letter: so I will bring it to an end.
  - Letter to Winifred Stevens (22 May 1887), p.197

- A bantam-hen that wastes an egg,
  Is sure to get extremely poor
  And to be forced at last to beg
  For hard-boiled eggs from door to door.
  - Letter to Violet Dodgson (6 May 1889), p.205

- I really didn't dare to send it across the Atlantic - the whales are so inconsiderate. They'd have been sure to want to borrow it to show to the little whales, quite forgetting that the salt water would be sure to ruin it.
    - Letter to <u>Isa Bowman</u>, with a copy of *Sylvie and Bruno*, (16 May 1890), p.214

- Do you know, I didn't even know of your *existence*? And it was *such* a surprise to hear that you had sent me your love! I felt just as if Nobody had suddenly run into the room, and given me a kiss! (That's the thing which happens to me, *most* days, just now.)
    - Letter to Sydney Bowlis (22 May 1891), p.221

- Don't forget the kiss to yourself, please; on the forehead is the best place.
    - Letter to Sydney Bowlis (22 May 1891), p.222

- I have very little time, now, fir society. (In fact, years ago, I began to decline *all* invitations.) The remaining years may be very few; and there is *much* work I still want to do.
    - Letter to Mrs. Egerton (8 March 1894), p.230

- Praise isn't good for any of us; love is, and it would be a good thing if all the world were full of it; I like my books to be loved, and I like to think some children love me for the books, but I don't like them praised.
    - Letter to "The Lowrie Children" (undated), pp.241-2

- I can guarantee that the books have no religious teaching whatever in them - in fact they do not teach anything at all.
    - Letter to "The Lowrie Children" (undated), p.242

- As to the meaning of the Snark? I'm very much afraid I didn't mean anything but nonsense!
    - Letter to "The Lowrie Children" (undated), pp.242-3

- In answer to your question, "What did you mean the Snark was?" will you tell your friend that I meant that the Snark was a *Boojum*. I trust that she and you will now feel quite satisfied and happy.
  - Letter to May Barber (12 Jan 1897), p.245

www.ingramcontent.com/pod-product-compliance
Lightning Source LLC
Chambersburg PA
CBHW070148230526
45471CB00002B/571